A Report of The Whole of The Proceedings Previous To, With a Note of The Evidence on, The Trial of Robert Keon, Gent. for The Murder of George Nugent Reynolds, Esq. And Also of the Charges of the Judges thereon. Together with The Arguments and Replies...

George Joseph Browne

A Report of The Whole of The Proceedings Previous To, With a Note of The Evidence on, The Trial of Robert Keon, Gent. for The Murder of George Nugent Reynolds, Esq. And Also of the Charges of the Judges thereon. Together with The Arguments and Replies of

A Report on the Trial of Robert Keon - 1788
George Joseph Browne
HAR03219
Monograph
Harvard Law School Library
Dublin: Printed by P. Byrne, No. 108, Grafton-Street. 1788

The Making of Modern Law collection of legal archives constitutes a genuine revolution in historical legal research because it opens up a wealth of rare and previously inaccessible sources in legal, constitutional, administrative, political, cultural, intellectual, and social history. This unique collection consists of three extensive archives that provide insight into more than 300 years of American and British history. These collections include:

Legal Treatises, 1800-1926: over 20,000 legal treatises provide a comprehensive collection in legal history, business and economics, politics and government.

Trials, 1600-1926: nearly 10,000 titles reveal the drama of famous, infamous, and obscure courtroom cases in America and the British Empire across three centuries.

Primary Sources, 1620-1926: includes reports, statutes and regulations in American history, including early state codes, municipal ordinances, constitutional conventions and compilations, and law dictionaries.

These archives provide a unique research tool for tracking the development of our modern legal system and how it has affected our culture, government, business – nearly every aspect of our everyday life. For the first time, these high-quality digital scans of original works are available via print-on-demand, making them readily accessible to libraries, students, independent scholars, and readers of all ages.

The BiblioLife Network

This project was made possible in part by the BiblioLife Network (BLN), a project aimed at addressing some of the huge challenges facing book preservationists around the world. The BLN includes libraries, library networks, archives, subject matter experts, online communities and library service providers. We believe every book ever published should be available as a high-quality print reproduction; printed on-demand anywhere in the world. This insures the ongoing accessibility of the content and helps generate sustainable revenue for the libraries and organizations that work to preserve these important materials.

The following book is in the "public domain" and represents an authentic reproduction of the text as printed by the original publisher. While we have attempted to accurately maintain the integrity of the original work, there are sometimes problems with the original work or the micro-film from which the books were digitized. This can result in minor errors in reproduction. Possible imperfections include missing and blurred pages, poor pictures, markings and other reproduction issues beyond our control. Because this work is culturally important, we have made it available as part of our commitment to protecting, preserving, and promoting the world's literature.

GUIDE TO FOLD-OUTS MAPS and OVERSIZED IMAGES

The book you are reading was digitized from microfilm captured over the past thirty to forty years. Years after the creation of the original microfilm, the book was converted to digital files and made available in an online database.

In an online database, page images do not need to conform to the size restrictions found in a printed book. When converting these images back into a printed bound book, the page sizes are standardized in ways that maintain the detail of the original. For large images, such as fold-out maps, the original page image is split into two or more pages

Guidelines used to determine how to split the page image follows:

• Some images are split vertically; large images require vertical and horizontal splits.
• For horizontal splits, the content is split left to right.
• For vertical splits, the content is split from top to bottom.
• For both vertical and horizontal splits, the image is processed from top left to bottom right.

from the _____ ✗

A

REPORT

OF THE WHOLE OF THE

PROCEEDINGS

PREVIOUS TO,

WITH A NOTE OF THE EVIDENCE

ON, THE

TRIAL

OF

ROBERT KEON, Gent.

FOR THE MURDER OF

GEORGE NUGENT REYNOLDS, Esq.

AND ALSO OF THE

Charges of the Judges thereon.

TOGETHER WITH

The *Arguments* and *Replies* of Counsel

ON THE MOTION IN

ARREST OF JUDGMENT;

AND THE

Decision of the Court thereon.

By *GEORGE JOSEPH BROWNE*,
BARRISTER AT LAW.

DUBLIN:
PRINTED BY P. BYRNE, No. 108, GRAFTON-STREET.
M.DCC.LXXXVIII.

E R R A T A.

Page 14, line 21—between the words *and*, and *appearing*, n-sert the words *two hundred and forty-two.*

Page 15, line 12—for *three hundred and sixty*—read *two hundred and forty-two.*

Page 27, line the laft—for *pieces of parchment which was figned at the laft*—read *pieces of parchment, there was but one fignature of the Sheriff, which was figned at the laft.*

Page 28, line 11—for *prifoners*—read *prifoner.*

Page 33, line 16—for *crimes*—read *crime.*

Page 125, line 15—for *29th*—read *19th.*

Page 126, line 9 from the bottom—for *more*—read *mere.*

Rec May 15, 1900

TO THE

RIGHT HONOURABLE

JOHN LORD BARON EARLSFORT,

LORD CHIEF JUSTICE OF IRELAND, &c. &c.

MY LORD,

THE following Report of a Case decided in that Court, where your Lordship presides at the head of the criminal jurisdiction of this kingdom, is now offered to the public, and is a better evidence of the patience, perspicuity, legal learning and sound ability, that at present adorn that Court, than whole volumes of panegyric.

As containing many points of criminal law which were very ingeniously argued at the bar, and very ably determined by the Bench, I trust it may be of some use to the profession, and therefore presume to inscribe it to your Lordship, in an humble confidence that it is not

utterly

utterly unworthy of your Lordfhip's protection ;
to attain which, fhall at all times be my moft
earneft ftudy, as in any degree to deferve it,
would be my greateft pride.

I have the honour to be,

My Lord,

your Lordfhip's moft obliged

grateful Servant,

GEO. JOS BROWNE.

Dublin, 18th *Feb.* 1788.

ADVERTISEMENT.

WHEN I was first retained as Counsel in the Case of the *King* and *Keon*, there was something in the circumstances on my instructions which excited my peculiar attention, and being in habits of taking notes, I resolved to set down the several facts which might take place at the Assizes. But when the Case came to be removed to the Court above, my attention became more eagerly interested, from my expectation of becoming professionally useful, as I knew that every thing that learning could explore, diligence discover, or ingenuity invent, was to be expected from the Gentlemen in the Defence, and when I reflected that Criminal Cases were not very frequent at the Bar of the Court of King's Bench in *Ireland*, I therefore thought that an accurate detail of the proceedings must be important to the Profession of the Law, and I, therefore, whether called on as a Barrister, or not, attended upon every motion that was made in the progress of the Case, and every argument that was had, until its conclusion. By my being thus engaged in the Case, I had the advantage of recurring to every Record, and perhaps, if I was not too negligent, or incapa-

ble,

ble, of the more eafily underftanding the fcope
of the arguments, and for the fame reafons I
have fet them forth, in this publication, at full
length

When I had looked over my Notes, which
were haftily enough arranged, I felt a confciouf-
nefs that the eloquence of fome, the ingenuity
of others, and the learning of all, had been much
injured by my efforts; yet, unwilling to lofe what
had coft me fome labour, I availed myfelf of the
friendfhip of the Gentlemen who argued this
Cafe. From them I have met the moft unre-
ferved affiftance, and if their arguments have
been put upon paper with any thing like the
force with which they appeared at the bar, it is
due to their revifion.

But though, upon this occafion, I have availed
myfelf of this affiftance, yet I feel it has been fo
great a drawback on the bufinefs of Gentlemen
of eminence in the profeffion, that I fhall not, in
any future publication of mine, trefpafs upon
their patience and emolument, with any revifion
of my labours, at the fame time that I fhall feel
myfelf honoured by the communication of the
arguments of gentlemen.

My intention, when I fet about this, was to
unite together the Records, the Facts, and the
Law

Law arifing from all, and therefore I poftponed any publication of the Trial until the motion in *arreft of judgment* fhould be finally decided upon, and though this publication was ready for the prefs fome time ago, yet as foon as I heard that a petition was preferred to the Lord Lieutenant, praying a *Writ* of *Error*, and was referred to his Majefty's Attorney-General, I determined that no part of the arguments fhould appear until the final decifion of the Cafe. That has now taken place; and I feel fome fort of pleafure, that if I fhall have committed any error in the latter part of my fubject, it will probably be fet right by the ability, induftry, and ingenuity of the two Gentlemen * who have already deferved fo well of their profeffion, by their *Reports* in the *King's Courts, Dublin*, and I am happy in the hope that by fuch *oppofite*, as well as *mutual* ftruggles, the profeffion may be benefited, and, according to Lord Bacon's motto to his Liber de Augmentis Scientiarum—" *Multi pertranfibunt & augebitur Scientia.*"

It may not be improper now to give fome reafon for the delay of my promifed *Reports* of *Cafes* in the *Court* of *King's Bench* in this

* Meffrs. Vernon and Scriven.

Kingdom,

Kingdom;—I had intended to publifh them in *Michaelmas Term* laft, but very early in that term I perceived, that the Cafes likely to be decided were fo few, that it would be moft prudent to enbody them with the Report of the Cafes of *Trinity Term*, and I do not hefitate to promife that I fhall, very early, lay them before the public, together with the Cafes which have been decided in the laft *Hilary Term*.

WHETHER I fhall either meet attention or protection for my induftry, was never a fubject which employed my thoughts I was always of opinion that every man owes fomething to his profeffion; and I know no man who has, in every way, been more indebted to mine than I have been, and I have had no other mode of repaying it, than by labour and if that fhall be deemed ufeful or advantageous to the profeffion, my ambition will be gratified, and my induftry overpaid.

GEO. JOS. BROWNE,

Dublin, 18*th Feb* 1788.

THE

THE

TRIAL, &c.

IN Spring Affizes, 1787, holden at *Carick-or Shannon*, for the county of *Leitrim*, before the Honourable James Fitzgerald, then his Majefty's fecond ferjeant at law, and the Honourable John Toler, then his Majefty's third ferjeant at law, the following bill of indictment was preferred againft Robert Keon, Ambrofe Keon, Edward Keon, Patrick Carty, and Michael Mullarky:

County of Leitrim, } THE Jurors of our faid Lord *to wit.* the King, upon their oaths prefent, that Robert Keon, late of Morea, in the county of Leitrim, Gent. Ambrofe Keon, late of Morea aforefaid, Gent. Edward Keon, late of the fame, E q, Patrick Carty, late of the fame, Yeoman, and Michael Mullarky, la'e of the fame, Gent. not having the fear of God before their eyes, but being moved and feduced by the inftigation of the Devil, on the fixteenth day of October, in the twenty-fixth year of the reign of our fovereign lord George the Third, now king of Great Bri-

A   tain,

tain, France and Ireland, and foforth, with force
and arms, at Drynaun, in the county of Leitrim
aforesaid, in and upon George Reynolds, otherwise George Nugent Reynolds, late of Litterfyan,
in the said county of Leitrim, Esq, in the peace
of God and our said lord the King, then and
there being, traiteroufly and feloniously and wilfully, and of their malice before-thought, did
make an affault, and that the said Robert Keon a
certain pistol, of the value of five shillings, then
and there charged with gun-powder and leaden
bullets, which pistol he the said Robert Keon in
his right hand then and there had and held to,
against, and upon the said George Reynolds,
otherwise George Nugent Reynolds, then and
there traiteroufly, feloniously, wilfully, and of
his malice before-thought, did shoot and difcharge, and that the said Robert Keon with the
leaden bullets aforefaid, out of the pistol aforefaid, then and there by force of the gun-powder
shot and fent forth as aforefaid, the aforefaid
George Reynolds, otherwise George Nugent Reynolds, in and upon the head of the said George
Reynolds, otherwife George Nugent Reynolds,
a little above the left eye-brow of him the said
George Reynolds, otherwife George Nugent Reynolds, then and there with the leaden bullets
aforefaid, out of the pistol aforefaid, by the said
Robert Keon fo as aforefaid, shot, difcharged and
fent, traiteroufly, feloniously, wilfully, and of his
malice before-thought, did strike, penetrate and
wound, giving the said George Reynolds, otherwife George Nugent Reynolds, with the leaden
bullets aforefaid, fo as aforefaid shot, difcharged,
and fent forth out of the pistol aforefaid by the
said Robert Keon, in and upon the said head of
him the said George Reynolds, otherwise George
Nugent Reynolds, a little above the left eye-
brow

brow of him the faid George Reynolds, otherwife George Nugent Reynolds, one mortal wound
of the depth of five inches, and of the breadth
of half an inch, of which faid mortal wound the
aforefaid George Reynolds, otherwife George
Nugent Reynolds, then and there inftantly died;
and that the aforefaid Ambrofe Keon, Edward
Keon, Patrick Carty, and Michael Mullarky,
then and there traiteroufly, felonioufly, wilful'y,
and of their malice before-thought were prefent, aiding, helping, abetting, comforting, af-
fifting and maintaining the faid Robert Keon to
kill and murder in manner and form aforefaid
the faid George Reynolds, otherwife George
Nugent Reynolds, then and there being a fubject
of our lord the King And fo the Jurors aforefaid upon their oaths aforefaid do fay, that the
faid Robert Keon, Ambrofe Keon, Edward Keon,
Patrick Carty, and Michael Mullarky, the faid
George Reynolds, otherwife George Nugent
Reynolds, then and there in manner and form
aforefaid, traiteroufly, felonioufly, wilfully, and
of their malice before-thought did kill and murder, againft the peace of our faid lord the King,
his crown and dignity, and againft the form of
the ftatute in that cafe made and provided.

Rex
versus
Keon.

TRUE BILL,

THO. TENISON and FELLOWS.

And the Grand Jury having fo found the above
to be a true bill, they were brought to the bar
on the fecond day of the affizes, and feverally
pleaded *Not Guilty*, and declared themfelves
ready for their trial ——On the next morning,
when they were ordered up, three affidavits were

sworn on behalf of the prisoners, for the purpose of putting off the trial, but were held insufficient by the Judge who presided on that occasion (Mr Serjeant Toler), and the pannel being
called over, there not appearing more than six-
teen Jurors, the Court ordered a *remanet* to be
entered *pro defectu juratorum*, remanding Robert
and Ambrose Keon, and admitting the other prisoners to bail.

The Counsel for the Crown, at the assizes,
were

Christopher Stone Williams,
John Kirwan,
John Geoghegan,   } Esquires.
George Joseph Browne,
And George Moore,

Solicitor, Ch. James Nisbett.

Counsel for the Prisoners.

John Blosset,
Toby Mulloy,
Ulick Burke,
Francis Paterson,
John Dillon,
John Peter Owen,
Edward King,   > Esquires.
James Whitestone,
Edmond Stanley,
Charles M'Carthy,
St George Daly,
Edward Carleton,
And Alexander Boyd,

Solicitor, Mr John Kelly.

N B. The several Jurors who made default
were fined 50*l.* each, and the Sheriff fined 500*l.*

19th

19th MAY, 1787   *B R.*

Rex
verfus
Keon.

Mr Attorney-General moved for a certiorari to be directed to the Judges of Aſſize for the county of Leitrim, the Clerk of the Crown of the ſaid county, or his deputy, to remove an indictment for murder.

Court —Be it ſo

16th JUNE, 1787.   *B. R.*

Mr Attorney-General moved for a habeas corpus to bring up the bodies of Robert Keon and Ambroſe Keon, then confined in the gaol of Carrick-on Shannon, in order to their being tried at the bar of this court, which was ordered accordingly, and afterwards Mr Stanley, Mr. Whiteſtone and Mr. Fox ſuggeſted to the Court, that Robert Keon was in ſuch a ſtate of health, that without iminent hazard to his life he could not be brought up, that therefore the iſſuing of the habeas corpus ought to be reſpited, and Browne, on the other ſide, having obſerved that this ſuggeſtion was not verified by any affidavit, this application was refuſed.

SATURDAY, JUNE 23, 1787.   *B. R.*

The Prime Serjeant* moved, that the record of the indictment in this cauſe might be remanded to the Clerk of the Crown, and that the iſſuing of the habeas corpus might be reſtrained, and if iſſued ſuperſeded This motion was founded on two affidaits of the bad ſtate of health of Robert

* James
Fitzgerald
Eſq, late
Second
Serjeant.

bert Keon, ſtating that he had a dropſy in his legs, and other dangerous complaints.

Mr Michael Smith made a ſimilar application on behalf of Ambroſe Keon ———They urged the inſuperable difficulty of being removed from the proper county where the facts were known, and the inconvenience of being continued in confinement ſo much longer than was neceſſary, for they could be tried at the next Summer Aſſizes, whereas by the rules of the Court they could not be tried at the bar before next Eaſter Term.

Court.———This buſineſs takes the lead of all others.

Mr. Fox, ſame ſide.—A foundation ought to be laid for a trial at Bar, that there was danger of not having an impartial trial, was it more probable to have a number of Jurors here than in the proper county.

Mr. Attorney General and Mr Geoghegan, on the other ſide —If juſtice could be attained at the aſſizes, there could be no objection to the motion, but it was impoſſible not to recollect what had already happened there On the firſt day of the aſſizes they were all, as they declared, ready for their trials, but on the next day they endeavoured to put them off by affidavits. And when the Court over-ruled the affidavits, though there was a pannel of more than eighty, ſcarcely any could be got to appear. It is ſworn that Robert Keon has a dropſical tendency, and that Ambroſe Keon is troubled with an indigeſ-tion and want of appetite. On the other hand they had a counter affidavit which ſtates, that ſo

far

far would a journey to town be from injuring them, that the Physician swore he believed it would be of advantage to their health.

Court —This case has been argued on wrong ground by the Counsel for the Keons; the question is not whether an impartial trial can be had, but whether there can be any trial at all if it be to be tried in the county of Leitrim. The removing of the Prisoners ought to be considered as a lenity to them. If they are in bad health, it removes from them the agitation arising from the expectation of a speedy trial. But though it was urged at the bar that they may be tried at the next assizes, it was assertion only, for there was no affidavit that they would be ready then to take their trial —What ground of hardship is there to be complained of? It had been confounded with the case of the Steel Boys, who had been tried by the Jury of another county.—If this case be of such magnitude, such a *Colossus* as to prevent a Jury from attending here or in the proper county, this Court must try whether the law is not too strong for the obstinacy or folly of a county of Leitrim Jury, who had set the law at defiance by a criminal apathy, and had stood out against trying the Prisoners. There was no hardship whatsoever in the Rule made, the Record was here, the Habeas Corpus had issued, and the Prisoners had near four months to take assistance from Physicians, in point of legal assistance they must also be bettered. In the case of the *King* against *Sheehy*, a popish priest, he was tried at the bar of this Court and acquitted; he was sent down to the county of Tipperary and convicted. So that in point of advantage the

Prisoners

Priſoners are bettered ; and in point of ſolemnity the Public.—The motion muſt be refuſed.

WEDNESDAY, JUNE 27th, 1787. *B. R.*

Mr Curran and Mr. Geoghegan moved that a day might be fixed for the trial of the Keons in the next term, all the Records being here, and the Return of the Habeas Corpus being out that day.

The Court appointed the ſecond Friday in the next Michaelmas Term.

Mr Geoghegan moved that the Sheriff might be directed to return the grand pannel.

The Court refuſed this application The Sheriff will return a Jury in the uſual way, and under the ordinary proceſs. *

---

* At the laſt Summer Aſſizes 1787, held for the county of Leitrim before the Honourable Mr Juſtice Crookſhank, and the Honourable Mr Juſtice Bennet, Edward Keon, Patrick Carty and Michael Mullarky ſurrendered themſelves in diſcharge of their bail, and the priſoners Robert and Ambroſe Keon being brought to the bar, the ſeveral proſecutors were bound over to a tend and give evidence againſt them at the bar of the Court of King's Bench on the 16th day of November following. The priſoners Robert Keon and Ambroſe Keon were remanded , and the other priſoners, Edward Keon, Patrick Carty and Michael Mullarky re-admitted to bail ; no objection having been made on behalf of the Crown. *Ut audivi.*

FRIDAY,

FRIDAY, NOVEMBER 16th, 1787. *B R.*

Rex
ver*sus*
Keon.

This day, purfuant to the order of Wednefday, June 27th, Robert Keon and Ambrofe
Keon, who had been brought up in the courfe
of the vacation, and committed to the gaol of
Newgate, and Edward Keon, Patrick Carty and
Michael Mullarky, who had furrendered themfelves in difcharge of their bail, were brought
up to the bar of this Court, and the Deputy
Clerk of the Crown proceeding to read a docket
of the Record *, the *Court* demanded why he

B   did

* *County of Leitrim*⎰ BE it remembered that at a general RECORD.
    to wit   ⎱ Affizes and general gaol delivery held at
————————— Carrick- n-Shannon, in the county of
Leitrim, in and for the faid county, the twenty-fixth day of
March, in the twenty-feventh year of the reign of our Sovereign Lord George the Third, now king of Great Britain and
foforth, and in the year of our Lord one thoufand feven hundred and eighty-feven, before the honourable James Fitz-
Gerald, Efq; his Majefty's Second Serjeant at Law for his
kingdom of Ireland, and the Honourable John Toler, his Majefty's Third Serjeant at Law for his faid kingdom of Ireland,
Juftices and Commiffioners of our faid Lord the King, affigned COMMIS
to hold all the Affizes, and alfo to hear difcufs, and determine all SION
and every treafons, murders, manflaughters, robberies, felonies,
unlawful affemblies, crimes, contempts, offences, evil doings,
and caufes whatfoever; and alfo affigned from time to time to
deliver the gaol of our faid Lord the King, of the county of
Leitrim aforefaid, of all the prifoners and malefactors therein
being, by virtue of a Commiffion of our faid Lord the King,
bearing date at Dublin the nineteenth day of February, in the
twenty-feventh year of the reign of our faid Lord the King
aforefaid, upon the oath of Thomas Tennifon, Efq; the GRAND
Right Honourable Owen Wynne, William Parfons Perc), Efq, JURY,
James Johnfton, Efq, Richard Cunningham, Efq, Thomas
Dickfon, Efq, Patrick Carter, Efq, Thomas Tennifon, jun
Efq; Launcelot Lawder, Efq; John Johnfon, Efq; Johnfton
                                    Morton

did not read the entire, he answered, that it was all that for the present was necessary, and then having received the pannel from John Peyton, Esq.

Morton, Esq, John Crofton, Esq, Richard Irwin, Esq; William Shanly, Esq, John Cullen, Esq, George Percy, Esq, Duke Crofton, Esq, John Carleton, Esq, Robert Johnson, Esq, Connolly Coen, Esq; John O'Brien, Esq, Coote Nisbett, Esq, William Slack, Esq, good and lawful men of the county of Leitrim aforesaid, which said Jurors being then and there duly impannelled, sworn and charged to enquire on behalf of our said Lord the King, and the body of the county of Leitrim aforesaid, of such matters, articles and things as were then and there enjoined them and given them in charge,

it is presented in manner and form following, that is to say, County of Leitrim, to wit The Jurors of our Lord the King, upon their oaths present, that Robert Keon, late of Morea, in the county of Leitrim, gentleman, Ambrose Keon, late of Morea aforesaid, gentleman; Edward Keon, late of the same, Esq, Patrick Carty, late of the same, yeoman, and Michael Mallarky, late of the same, gentleman, not having the fear of God before their eyes, but being moved and seduced by the instigation of the devil, on the sixteenth day of October, in the twenty sixth year of the reign of our Sovereign Lord George the Third, now King of Great Britain, France and Ireland, and soforth, with force and arms, at Drinawn, in the county of Leitrim aforesaid, in and upon George Reynolds, otherwise George Nugent Reynolds, late of Littersyan in the county of Leitrim, Esq, in the peace of God and of our said Lord the King, then and there being, traiterously and feloniously and wilfully, of their malice aforethought, did make an assault, and that the said Robert a certain pistol of the value of five shillings, then and there charged with gunpowder and leaden bullets, which pistol he the said Robert Keon in his right hand then and there had and held, to, against, and upon the said George Reynolds, otherwise George Nugent Reynolds, then and there traiterously, feloniously, wilfully, and of his malice beforethought, did shoot and discharge, and that the said Robert Keon, with the leaden bullets aforesaid, out of the pistol aforesaid, then and there by force of the gunpowder, shot and sent forth as aforesaid, the aforesaid George Reynolds, otherwise George Nugent Reynolds, in and upon the head of the said George Reynolds, otherwise George Nugent Reynolds, a little above the left eye-brow of him

Efq, High Sheriff of the county of Leitrim, he read the following Return — " The execution of the within Writ appears by certain " pannels hereunto annexed—So anſwers John " Peyton, Sheriff"

B 2

The

him the ſaid George Reynolds, otherwiſe George Nugent Reynolds, then and there, with the leaden bullets aforeſaid, out of the piſtol aforeſaid, by the ſaid Robert Keon to a aforeſaid ſhot, diſcharged and ſent forth, traiterouſly, feloniouſly, willfully and of his malice aforethought, did ſtrike, penetrate and wound, giving the ſaid George Reynolds, otherwiſe George Nugent Reynolds, with the leaden bullet aforeſaid, ſo as aforeſaid ſhot, diſcharged, and ſent forth out of the piſtol aforeſaid by the ſaid Robert Keon, in and upon the head of him the ſaid George Reynolds, otherwiſe George Nugent Reynolds, a little above the left eye-brow of him the ſaid George Reynolds, otherwiſe George Nugent Reynolds, one mortal wound of the depth of five inches, and of the breadth of half an inch, of which ſaid mortal wound the aforeſaid George Reynolds, otherwiſe George Nugent Reynolds, then and there inſtantly died; and that the aforeſaid Ambroſe Keon, Edward Keon, Patrick Carty, and Michael Mullarky, then and there traiterouſly, feloniouſly, wilfully, and of their malice beforethought, were preſent, aiding, helping, abetting, comforting, aſſiſting and maintaining the ſaid Robert Keon to kill and murder, in manner and form aforeſaid, the ſaid George Reynolds, otherwiſe George Nugent Reynolds, then and there being a ſubject of our ſaid Lord the King; and ſo the Jurors aforeſaid, upon their oaths aforeſaid, do ſay that the ſaid Robert Keon, Ambroſe Keon, Edward Keon, Patrick Carty, and Michael Mullarky, the ſaid George Reynolds, otherwiſe George Nugent Reynolds, then and there, in manner and form aforeſaid, traiterouſly, feloniouſly, and wilfully, and of their malice beforethought, did kill and murder, againſt the peace of our ſaid Lord the King, his crown and dignity, and againſt the form of the Statute in that caſe made and provided. Whereupon the ſaid Robert Keon, Ambroſe Keon, Michael Mullarky, Edward Keon, and Patrick Carty, in their proper perſons, then and there came before the Juſtices and Commiſſioners aforeſaid, under the cuſtody of John Peyton, Eſq; Sheriff of the County of Leitrim aforeſaid, to whoſe cuſtody they, the ſaid Robert Keon, Ambroſe Keon, Michael Mullarky, Edward Keon, and Patrick Carty, for the crime aforeſaid, were before

that

Rex
verſus
Keon

The names of the perſons returned on the pannel were then called over, and two hundred and forty-two having appeared, the priſoners were aſked by the Deputy Clerk of the Crown, if they joined in their challenges. *Mr. Write-ſtone*, of Counſel for the priſoners, moved to have the * *Certiorari, Return* thereon, and the *Venire*

that time committed, being brought to the Bar of the ſaid Court, in cuſtody as aforeſaid, and forthwith being demanded concern-ing the premiſes in the ſaid Indictment above ſpecified, and charged upon them, how they will acquit themſelves thereof, they ſay, and each of them ſayeth, that he is not guilty thereof, and thereof for good and evil they ſeverally put themſelves

PLEA, not
guilty

ISSUE

AWARD of
Venire

upon the Country, and William Chapman, Eſq; Clerk of the Crown and Coroner of our ſaid Lord the King, who for our ſaid Lord the King, in this behalf, doth proſecute, doth the like, and ſoforth, which ſaid Indictment, with all things touching the ſame, our ſaid Lord the King, for certain reaſons, cauſed to come before him to be determined (Therefore to try the iſſue aforeſaid, in manner aforeſaid, joined, the Sheriff of the County of Leitrim is commanded that he do not omit, and ſoforth, but that he cauſe to come before the ſaid Lord the King, on Friday next, after the Morrow of Saint Martin next coming, wherefoever and ſoforth, twelve and ſoforth, by whom and ſoforth, and who neither and ſoforth, to recognize and ſo-forth, becauſe as well and ſoforth, the ſame day is given as well to the ſaid William Chapman, Eſq; Coroner and Attorney of our ſaid Lord the King, who for our ſaid Lord the King in this behalf proſecutes, who and ſoforth, as to the ſaid Robert Keon, the ſaid Ambroſe Keon, the ſaid Michael Mullarky, the ſaid Edward Keon, and the ſaid Patrick Carty, there and ſoforth)

CERTIO-
RARI

* GEORGE the Third by the Grace of God of Great Britain, France and Ireland, King Defender of the Faith, and ſoforth To our juſtices of aſſize and general gaol delivery, held for the county of Leitrim, the Clerk of the Crown of the ſaid county, or his deputy there greeting We being de-ſirous for certain reaſons that there ſhould be truly certified un-to us, the cauſes of all and ſingular inquiſitions, preſentments, indictments or recognizances, remaining in your cuſtody or in the cuſtody of any of you, wherein Robert Keon, Edward Keon,

Venire read   They were read accordingly; and Mr Whiteftone then was going to object to them, when the Court informed him that they could hear no objections now, and that he would have

Keon, Ambrofe Keon, Michael Mullarky, and Patrick Carty, ftand indicted or prefented of any treafon or murder, or any fuch like offence, or by whatfoever other name, fur-name, or addition of name or fur-name, the faid Robert Keon, Ambrofe Keon, Edward Keon, Michael Mullarky, and Patrick Carty, are efteemed or called in the fame   We therefore command you and every of you, that the faid inquifitions, prefentments, indictments, and recognizances, with all things touching the fame, in as full and ample a manner as the fame remains in your cuftody, or in the cuftody of any of you, to us on Friday next after the Morrow of the Holy Trinity next coming, wherefoever we fhall then be in Ireland, diftinctly and plainly, do fend under your feals or the feals of any of you, together with this writ, that we may infpect the premifes, and caufe further to be done thereupon, what fhall appear to us of right according to the laws and cuftoms of this our kingdom of Ireland ought to be done   Witnefs John Lord Earlsfort, at the Kings Courts, the twenty-firft day of May, in the twenty-feventh year of our reign.

NISBITT, *Attorney.*   C A R T E R.

By the Court for the King.

(Allowed) E A R L S F O R T.

TO our Sovereign Lord the King within named, I moft humbly certify that the execution of the within Writ to me directed, appears by a certain record, indictment, examinations and inquifitions hereunto annexed.

So anfwers

W I L L I A M C H A P M A N,

CLERK CROWN.

(SEAL)

[14]

Rex
verfus
Keon.

have four days to move upon after the trial, and might then avail his client of any objections to the record when made up.

An affidavit was then sworn by the prisoner, Robert Keon

The Prime Serjeant ——This I apprehend is the proper time for me to make use of that licence which the Crown has been graciously pleased to grant me, and to make an application on behalf of the unfortunate gentleman at your bar, who for thirteen months has been the most oppressed, traduced, and misrepresented man living, and yet from the conduct of his profecutors, he feels himself obliged to throw himself upon the justice of the Court, and to defire to postpone to a future day the vindication of his character, dearer though it is to him than life itself The appearance of the Jury upon this occasion speaks more loudly than volumes of affidavits could A pannel of three hundred and sixty returned and appearing, is so unusual and unprecedented, that every man must start at its novelty. It has in fact put the nomination of the Jury in the power of his profecutors, and made the statute of Edward * a nullity This practice would be more grievous to the subject than that which the statute intended to correct. The prisoners must go through the whole of the pannel before the profecutor can be called upon to assign any cause of challenge, and by that means the profecutor has a kind of election or nomination of the Jury, or rather *a veto* upon every man returned ——There are some prizes, it is true, and very rich ones in this pannel, but of these the profecutor can deprive the unfortunate

* 33 Ed 1 st 4.

nate

nate prifoner, and leave him in fo large a number
of blanks, that he muft rifk every thing dear to
the feelings of a man—his life and his honour—
The Sheriff is a gentleman highly honourable,
and he, I am fure, would not have made fuch
a return, if he did not think himfelf at once
vindicating the honour of his country, and com-
plying with the direction of the Court ——The
Court gave no direction —It has been rumoured
that a Jury could not be had at the laft affizes
for the trial of the prifoner in the vicinage, and
now three hundred and fixty Jurors appear at
your bar, one hundred miles diftant from their
country—the poifon intermediately adminiftered
by the profecutors has operated.   The paffions
of the country have been inflamed—and by fuch
means—but let the affidavit fpeak for itfelf ——
It ftates that ever fince the death of the late
George Nugent Reynolds, the profecutors have
ufed their moft earneft endeavours to prejudice
the minds of the people againft the prifoner Robert Keon, the appearance of the Jury proves
with what fuccefs—It ftates that the public
mind would have been otherwife fair, calm and
difpaffionate —It ftates, that fhortly after the
death of George Nugent Reynolds, an inflammatory ballad was by the procurement of the
profecutors compofed and circulated through the
county of Leitrim, wherein the prifoner's name,
being Keon, he is compared to Cain who committed the firft murder   It ftates the republica-
tion of this ballad in this city on the eve of this
trial, and the finging of it through that quarter
of this city in which the county of Leitrim has
depofited itfelf for the prefent occafion. It ftates
that feveral of the prifoner's witneffes have been
fpirited away—that private inquifitions have been
held,

Rex
versus
Keon

held that the witnesses have often rehearsed their parts, and would now come forward confident in their fictitious confistency, and the absence of those who, if not spirited away would be forthcoming to contradict them. Upon the ground of this affidavit calling loudly for an answer, and the few authorities I cite, I trust the Court will postpone the trial ——In the case of

* 1 Bur. 510.

the King and Martha Grey,* the Richmond Park Case, the Court put off the trial in consequence of libels circulated to prejudice the Jury— In the Case of the King and Brownrigg, at the Old Baily, the trial was postponed on the same principle——In the Case of the Dean of Saint Asaph, the trial was to have been before Sir Lloyd Kenyon, and it was put off because several extracts from Locke, Doctor Towers, and others, recommending the principles of the original libel, had been printed, and circulated thro' the country for the purpose of influencing the Ju-

*See printed trial.

ry.*If the trial be postponed, no difficulty can ensue, it can only delay, not elude justice, whereas if the unfortunate prisoner shall, under the circumstances stated, be ordered upon his trial, it will be impossible for the Court to redress him.— Better, says the law, it is that ninety-nine guilty should escape, than one innocent man should suffer—Your Lordships surely will give the fever some time to subside I, for my own part, have ever been of opinion, that applications on behalf of a prosecutor and a prisoner, to postpone trials, stood upon different grounds— the prisoner desires it at an high price, the possible relinquishment of the advantage of the cross examination of the witnesses against him, and the death of his own, whereas, by the information given, the evidence of the prosecution is as it

were

were perpetuated, and if the witnesses should die, the information may be made use of against the Prisoner, without the advantage of a cross examination Your Lordships may remand the Record, as was done in the case of the King against Kilduff, under Lord Anally's Act, or you may appoint a trial at bar in the next term; it will be but a delay of a few days, a delay consistent with the principles of the law ——In reproach of the worst days of the Roman Empire, the satyrist says, " *De morte hom nis nulla cunctatio longa est* " But the law of England says, " That where the life of a man is concerned all possible deliberation should be had " In the interval which is desired, the effect of those dangerous and inflammatory libels will die away, the witnesses of the Prisoner may possibly be recovered, the public mind will have time to cool, and will subside into a temperate disposition and a calm spirit of investigation and enquiry.

Rex n versus Keon.

The affidavit was then read, which was in substance as stated by the Prime Serjeant.

Mr *Recorder* * stated that the other prisoners were ready to abide their trials

Denis George, Esq.

Lord *Earlsfort* —We are all agreed in the Rule to be made, and it is impossible not to observe, both on the time and the manner in which the affidavit was made. It was handed to the prisoner in the presence of the Court, and he read it, and swore it In a case of such consequence, so many futile objections have been scarcely ever made. The Court is sworn to do justice between the crown and the subject, were it not, and if it could be moved, it had been

C   better

better it had not been read. The pannel is said to be too large The five prisoners have been asked would they join in their challenges should the Court permit them to sever, they may challenge one hundred, and does not this alone shew the necessity of a large pannel If after thirteen months confinement, and an appearance of two hundred and forty-two freeholders, an impartial and unprejudiced Jury cannot be had, it never can If an unprejudiced Jury cannot be found in that number, can it be found in forty ?—If thirteen months has not given time for men to become cool, their minds never will cool —Why is this cause here ? Is it because the minds of those who might be on the Jury might be heated ? No No Jury could be had to gratify their feelings —If there were any leaning, it was on the other side. They abandoned the dignity of justice, and permitted the prisoners to go untried It is objected that inflammatory publications have been dispersed. Is there any time in which some friend of the prisoner may not disperse these wretched publications ?—*Sir Fletcher Norton* was once well set down by a Juror, on a complaint made by him of papers dispersed against his client , the Juror drily said, " I have got a paper on the other " side " They are called in this miserable production, " beasts of prey." Could any thing like this influence the meanest freeholder ? No ; the mind of every man would revolt against such ribaldry The inference to be drawn from this kind of charge is, that while a ballad-monger exists no criminal is to be tried. *Brownrigg*'s case is cited, as an authority for postponing a trial on account of publications. That was an *Old Bailey* case, where the sessions occurred
quickly

quickly after the fact. This has happened more than twelve months ago, and in such a period of time every man must have approached the facrament. *Martha Grey*'s cafe was alfo cited, it is as far from *Martha Grey*'s cafe, as from any thing in the books. That was an angry cafe between the *Crown* and the *fubject*, not as the name of the *Crown* is affumed for the *Juftice* of the country in every criminal profecution. As it was well obferved by Queen Elizabeth to Lord *Bacon*, when he as Attorney General told her Majefty that he was " *qui pro Domina Regina* " *profequitur* " Not " *Domina Regina*," replied the Queen, in the true fpirit of the conftitution, but " *Domina Juftitia* " In *Martha Grey*'s cafe *Richmond Park* had been fhut up, and a fubfcription had been fet on foot to prevent its continuing fo. The firft opener of that popular bufinefs was a cobler, who, poffeffed of the noble fpirit of the conftitution which adorns that bold and gallant people, excited them to preferve an ancient privilege. Thefe two of the principal profecutors were by affidavit charged with having procured the libel to be written, publifhed and delivered. Here, for any thing appears, the publication was by the friends of the prifoner himfelf — There is one reafon, and one only, that has a colour of weight with it, and that is, that the witneffes for the prifoner have been fpirited away, but what fact is there to ground this general affertion—The names of witneffes are not mentioned, nor is it afferted that Crown fummonfes have been at all iffued, nor has the place of their abode been at all afcertained, nor any reafon given why their attendance was not procured. Thefe are the principal objections; and is there any of them that takes this from out

C 2   the

the Rule in Foster,* where it is said that affidavits, even in High Treason, ought to be sparingly admitted It is said that Judges ought to be Council for the prisoners—so they ought—Why?—for the sake of justice. But were the Court now to postpone the trial, would it be justice? Thirteen months have elapsed since the fact has taken place. The Court cannot keep witnesses alive Besides, if the party complained of is so powerful, witnesses may be tampered with. It may be necessary to observe to these who hear the Court, that it is not because they hear a man accused of a crime that they are therefore to believe him guilty —No. God forbid—for the dignity of human nature, they ought to think him otherwise. Thus much might be proper to observe, least any person who might be on the Jury should have paid any attention to the affidavit It had been suggested that the Court might remand him If it did, perhaps there might again be no Jury, it was therefore the opinion of the Court that the trial should now go on, and not compel the Sheriff perhaps a second time to bring up so large a number of freeholders from the county of Leitrim.

Mr. *Recorder* then said he meant on behalf of the prisoners to challenge the Array. The foundation of his challenge was, that the Sheriff had returned too many on the pannel. And he here prayed that the *Venire* and *Return* thereon might be read, and the Council for the Crown not objecting, they were read accordingly The *Court* demanded, would the prisoners join in their challenges. Mr. *Recorder* answered they would not.

The *Court*.—Then try Robert Keon alone.

Mr.

Mr *Recorder* then tendered the following
Challenge

The King against Robert | AND now, here the
Keon, Gentleman, Am- | said Robert Keon in his
brose Keon, Edward | proper person, comes and
Keon, Patrick Carty, | prays oyer of the said
and Michael Mullarky | writ of *venire facias* and
——————————— | the return thereto, and
they are read to him in the words following:
" George the Third, by the Grace of God, of
" Great Britain, France, and Ireland, King, De-
" fender of the Faith and so forth, to the She-
" riff of the county of Leitrim greeting. We
" command you that you omit not for any li-
" berty within your bailiwick, but that you cause
" to come before us on Friday next after the
" morrow of St Martin next coming, wherefo-
" ever we shall then be in Ireland, twelve free
" and lawful men of the body of your county,
" every of whom shall have forty shillings ster-
" ling at least in lands, tenements, or rents, by
" whom the truth of the matter may be better
" known, and who are in no wise related either
" to William Chapman, Esq, Coroner and Attor-
" ney of our said Lord the King, of the county
" of Leitrim, who for our said Lord the King
" in this behalf prosecutes, and Robert Keon,
" Ambrose Keon, Edward Keon, Patrick Carty,
" and Michael Mullarky, to consider upon their
" oath, if they the said Robert Keon, Ambrose
" Keon, Edward Keon, Patrick Carty, and Mi-
" chael Mullarky, be guilty of a certain trea-
" son and murder whereof they stand indicted,
                              " because

Rex
versus
Keon.

" becaufe the faid William Chapman, Attorney
" and Coroner of our faid Lord the King of our
" county of Leitrim, who for our faid Lord the
" King in this behalf profecutes, and the faid
" Robert Keon, Ambrofe Keon, Edward Keon,
" Patrick Carty, and Michael Mullarky, between
" whom the contention is, have put themfelves
" thereof on that jury, and have you then there the
" names of that jury and this Writ Witnefs, John
" Lord Earlsfort, at the King's Courts, the twen-
" ty-feventh day of June, in the twenty-feventh

Return.
" year of our reign. The execution of the with-
" in writ appears by certain *pannels* hereunto
" annexed. So anfwers John Peyton, Sheriff "
Which faid pannel being read, Robert Keon
prays judgment of the faid return and of the array of the Jurors aforefaid, and that the fame
may be quafhed, and for caufes of challenge he
fets down, and doth affign to the Court of our
Lord the King the caufes following · That the
faid Sheriff of the county of Leitrim hath returned to the *venire* aforefaid, the names of three
hundred and twenty-eight perfons as and for a
Jury to try the iffue aforefaid, which are a greater number of Jurors than according to the laws
and cuftoms of the realm ought to have been returned to the *venire* aforefaid, and for that it appears by the faid Sheriff's return to the faid writ
of *venire facias*, that he hath annexed certain pannels to the faid writ of *venire facias* Whereas
by law he ought to have returned but one pannel,
and one Jury thereto, and for that the faid array
of the Jurors aforefaid, and the return to the faid
writ of *venire facias* is altogether illegal and wants
form , wherefore for the feveral caufes aforefaid,
the

the faid Robert prays judgment of the faid array of the Jurors aforefaid, and of the return of the writ of *venire facias*, and that the fame may be quafhed, and foforth.

Rex
verfus
Keon.

DENIS GEORGE.

Mr *Duquery*, on behalf of the Crown, de-murred

Mr. *Recorder*, for the prifoner, joined in demurrer, and then argued that this was a joint *venire* to try five prifoners, though it directs twelve Jurors to try the iffue. He ad-mitted that the Sheriff might return twenty-four at common law, and that at this day he is not limited to return any number in particular, but within the memory of man there had not been fuch a Return as the prefent one, this Return in fact deprived the prifoner of the benefit of the law, and gave the Crown in effect the fame thing as an indefinite right of challenge without caufe, and fo the Court will not fay that fuch an array can be legal. This is a trial at bar, and the pri-foner could not, as if the trial were in the proper county, have his witneffes ready to prove fuch of his caufes of challenge as the Juror himfelf may not be examined to, but found in his re-proach The Sheriff in his Return has faid, that he has arrayed the Jury in certain pannels to the *venire* annexed But the Sheriff cannot return feveral and diftinct *pannels* upon a joint *venire* If it were a matter of property of but ten pounds value only, there would be one pannel and one Jury, here the Sheriff fays that he has returned feveral *pannels* on one joint *venire*, but it may be faid that he has returned but one piece
of

of parchment, one roll, though he has called it *pannels*, or in other words, he has said one thing and done another, but the utmost credit is due to his return, and as he has said he returned *pannels*, and but one appears, there must have been some diminution since. The question resolves itself into this—he returned several pannels, or he did not, if he has returned several pannels, he has done wrong, and something is suppressed, if he has not, then he has made a false return, and either way it is fatal. If there be several pannels, each must have been authenticated by the Sheriff's name, and that for these reasons the Challenge ought to be allowed, and the Array quashed.

Mr *Stanley*, on the same side, contended on the authority of Co Littleton, 135, * that no more than twenty-four Jurors were returnable at common law on any issue on a common *venire facias*. That in the Commission of Gaol Delivery the Court proceeded to award a pannel without writ or precept, but that was not as in the present case where the Court sat in another county, trying a foreign indictment removed by Certiorari. That permitting so great a number would be effectually repealing the statute of 33d Edward I which restrains the power of the Crown as to challenging without cause shewn. When Mr Spencer Cowper was tried for the murder of Sarah Stout * there were only forty-eight Jurors returned on the pannel. He contended that

* State Tr. V. 94.

* Mr Stanley has since informed me that there was a mistake of a figure in the above quotation, as made by him, for that he had intended to have cited Co Littleton 155.

that Lord Hale expresfly lays it down, that on a
Venire Facias the Court can award but twenty-
four Jurors, and if the prifoner fhould challenge
fo many that a fufficient number fhould not be
left on the original pannel, a writ of *Decem or Octo
tales* might be awarded as at common law—That
no inconvenience whatfoever could arife from
quafhing the array, for under Lord Annaly's
Act, 22d George III the record might be remanded and the prifoners tried in the country.
——For this he cited the Cafe of the King and
Killduff, when Lord Earlsfort was Attorney General, which cafe had been removed by Certiorari from the county of Rofcommon, and was
afterwards removed *pro Defectu Juratorum,*
and tried before Lord Chief Juftice Carleton,
then Solicitor General, and the prifoner was convicted.

Mr. *O'Connor* on the fame fide, cited Sir
Harry Vane's Cafe, * as to the number of Jur- * Kelynge
ors 16

Mr *Calbeck*, for the Crown—In fupport of the
demurer faid, that the gentlemen on the other
fide were confounding civil and criminal cafes
—If the doctrine laid down by them were admitted, there never could be a criminal trial at
bar, for if the prifoner challenged twenty he
could not be tried by four In civil cafes the
party has no peremptory challenges, in them a
return of thirty-fix would be a fufficient return,
for if each fide challenged twelve, there would
remain twelve to try the iſſue Every cafe that
had been tried at the bar of that Court had been
an authority for him.

D   *Beare.*

Rex
verfus
Keon
6 St. Tr.

Bennet, J.—Cited *Layer's* cafe where the point was made but given up

Mr *Calaleck* called on the gentlemen on the other fide to fhew an inftance of a *decem tales* in a criminal cafe.—As to the other objection, that the fheriff had made ufe of the word *pannels* inftead of *pennel*, he wifhed that gentlemen would advert to the meaning of words, what is a *pannel*? It is in fact and truth no other than a fchedule annexed to the writ, and would it matter if the fheriff had faid fchedules or fchedule; *panella* is a little fquare piece of parchment, and the fheriff is not by the writ directed to return pannels but the names of men as Jurors.

Mr *Duquery* on the fame fide, would not prefs any thing on the Court in a capital cafe if he did not apprehend that the objections on the other fide were futile—for if they are of any validity, the prifoner may avail himfelf of them either by motion in arreft of judgment, or by writ of error.—All trials were originally at the bar of the Court, and if the powers of the Court of King's Bench were co-extenfive with the Courts of gaol delivery, there was an end of the objection—Juftices of gaol delivery were only an emanation of this Court. Mr *Duquery* was going on when he was ftopped by the Court

Lord *Earlfort* pronounced the opinion of the Court on the challenge—The fheriff may return *inftanter* at the affizes, but not as has been ftated from the bar, as often as he pleafes.—In the *Whiteboy* cafes, he had himfelf made the objection

jection as being an evasion of the statute of Edward I. If what was proposed were to be acceded to and the sheriff were to go on, as has been done, the trial would be postponed for ever. If the legislature could have supposed the number of Jurors could ever be too large, they would have restrained the number. The statute enacts, that persons from the neighbourhood shall be returned, but does not say how many, but that the sheriff shall not return too many.—Apply the statutes to the present case, if ever there were a case where a complaint was made of the Jury being too large he declared himself to be a stranger to it. The writ directs the sheriff to return twelve and it is admitted that he may return twenty-four, surely by a return of twenty-four he as much transgresses the exigency of the writ, as if he had returned four hundred.—The sheriff is directed it is contended to return no more than twenty-four, if the prisoner challenges twenty, then there remain only four, and the prisoner never can be tried.—The absurdity of this position appears from this. It is contended that the prisoner is injured by too large a pannel—how? because from the number there is a fear of a defect of Jurors.—The prisoner has twenty challenges, does a large pannel prevent that?—certainly not,—when the pannel is gone through the Crown is to shew its causes of challenge, until a fair Jury can be had. In the case of the *King* against *Sheehy*, in which I was concerned, there the pannel was as it ought to be an ample one. As to the other objection that the sheriff has used the word pannels instead of pannel, it cannot by any distortion be presumed that there are several pannels there being but one return, even if there were several pannels or pieces of parchment, which was signed at the

last.

last   There is no foundation for the one or the other objection, the prisoner, however, will be able to avail himself of these objections if there be any thing in them, as they will appear on the face of the record.

Per Curiam—The trial must go on.

Mr *Prime Serjeant*, on behalf of the prisoner, Robert Keon, objected to his being tried separately from the other prisoners.

The Clerk of the Crown then called upon the prisoners and prosecutors to look to their challenges.

And the Jury was called, and they were sworn or challenged as follows

John Gore, Esquire,	sworn.
William Gore, Esquire,	informed the Court that his health rendered him unable to attend, he was set by.
Sir Edward Newenham	stated to the Court that he was unable to hear the evidence accurately, he was set by.
Morgan Crofton, Esquire, challenged peremptorily.	
Robert Ford, Esquire,	objected to as not residing in the county, and 2 *Hawk* cap. 43, sect. 26, was cited to shew that to be a good cause of challenge, Lord Earlsfort

Earlsfort directed Mr Ford to ſtand by, tho' he apprehended if a Juror ſo diſqualified be returned and appear, it is no cauſe of challenge.

Pat Dundas,   challenged for affinity to the deceaſed He was examined on oath, and that challenge overruled ; and he was then challenged peremptorily.

Robert Whitelaw,   challenged as being upon the Coroner's Inqueſt , put by.

Francis Johnſon,   challenged peremptorily.

Andrew Johnſon,   challenged peremptorily.

John Carter,   challenged peremptorily.

John Hamilton,   challenged peremptorily.

William Moſtyn,   challenged peremptorily.

Thomas Gregg,   challenged peremptorily.

Corn O'Brien,   ſet by.

Henry Griffith,   challenged peremptorily.

Edward Hamilton,   challenged peremptorily.

Thomas Webſter,   challenged peremptorily.

Edward O'Brien,   ſet by

Edward Wilſon,   ſet by.

Francis Slack,   challenged for affinity, which he having admitted

	ted on his examination on oath, he was difcharged.
William Armftrong,	challenged peremptorily.
Robert Aljeo,	challenged for having given an opinion in the cafe, and Robert Whitelaw being examined as to that fact, Aljeo was difcharged.
Chriftopher Lawder,	the like challenge , and Myles Keon, Efq, examined, who proved that Mr. Lawder had faid, that if he were upon Mr Keon's trial, he muft find him guilty. Lawder was accordingly difcharged.
John Carlton,	fet by
Thomas Kerr,	challenged by the prifoner for want of freehold , *which he being fworn to the fact, and having admitted*, was difcharged.
William Tredenick,	challenged peremptorily.
William Hamilton,	challenged peremptorily.
John King,	fworn.
Francis Waldron,	fet by.
James Dixon,	challenged peremptorily
James O'Neil,	fet by.
William Philips,	fworn.

James

James Veaitch,	challenged peremptorily.	Rex *versus* Keon
John Parke,	set by.	
John Phibbs,	challenged for cause ; that he was hard of hearing, and the fact appearing to the Court, he was discharged.	
Garret Tyrrell,	sworn.	
William Lawder,	challenged peremptorily.	
Richard Lockart,	challenged peremptorily.	
John Morton,	challenged for having made declarations, and being sworn, acknowledged that he had said *if on the Jury* he must find him guilty ; discharged.	
John Whitelaw,	challenged as having been on the Inquest, which being admitted, it was allowed a good challenge, and he was discharged.	
Price Simpson,	set by.	
Newcomen Whitelaw,	challenged for relationship to Mr Reynolds, which he on being sworn having admitted, he was discharged	
Samuel Walker,	challenged peremptorily.	
Lewis Aljeo,	sworn.	
John Nichols,	set by	
John Lowe	sworn.	

Simon

Rex *versus* Keon.	Simon Armstrong,	sworn.
	Glaude Moore,	sworn.
	Robert Reycraft,	challenged for cause, his having made declarations as to the guilt of the prisoner. Mr. John Gore was examined, who having proved the declarations, Mr. Reycraft was discharged.
	Richard Jones	set by
	William Hamilton,	set by.
	Thomas Berry,	challenged for cause; his having made declarations as to the guilt of the prisoner Mr Fra. Keon was examined, who having proved the declarations, Mr. Berry was discharged
	Robert Atkinson,	challenged for cause; declarations made as to the guilt of the prisoner, but not being able to prove them, Mr. Atkinson was sworn.
	Henry Scott,	challenged for declarations, which he on his own examination on oath admitted, he was discharged.
	Thomas Trenor,	sworn.
	Samuel Crawford,	sworn
	John Ball,	sworn.

The

The Clerk of the Crown then called over the Names of the Jury, as follows

Rex verſus Keon.

John Gore,	Simon Armſtrong,
John King,	Glaude More,
William Philips,	Robert Atkinſon,
Carret Tyrrel,	Thomas Trenor,
Lewis Aljeo,	Samuel Crawford,
John Lowe,	John Ball.

The Clerk of the Crown then read the Indictment, and gave the Priſoner, Robert Keon, in charge to the above Jury.

Mr *Duquery* —It is my duty, as Counſel for the Crown, however painful the diſcharge of that duty may be, to lay before you, as conciſely as poſſible, the nature and circumſtances of the crimes with which the priſoner ſtands charged, and for which he is now to take his trial at your bar

When Counſel ſtate caſes of this nature, I conceive it to be their office to diſcloſe to the Court and the Jury, with as much clearneſs and preciſion as they can, the facts which they are inſtructed will appear in proof, in order to elucidate the evidence which is to be produced, and to point your attention to the material parts of the caſe, but I do not conceive it to be by any means the province of Counſel to endeavour to exaggerate the facts, or to awaken the paſſions of the Jury   Whatever profeſſional ability and addreſs may be exerted on other occaſions, in caſes of this nature the ingenuity of the advocate muſt be totally laid aſide, and nothing ſtated as a fact which is not founded in the proofs, nor

E   any

any thing advanced as law, which cannot be ftrongly fupported

If the Counfel for the profecution know of any circumftance favourable to the prifoner, they fhould unfold it as readily, and as fully, as any matter which they may urge in fupport of the charge The Crown and the public can have no intereft but in the conviction of the *Guilty:* The punifhment even of the offender is only the fecondary object of the law, the prevention of crimes is the firft. It cannot therefore be the wifh of thofe concerned for the profecution to endeavour to miflead the Jury from the truth, or to draw down the penalties of the law upon any man who does not juftly merit its punifh-ment. The charge which is brought againft the prifoner at the bar is not advanced on any light prefumption If he be not really guilty of the crime imputed to him, thofe who accufe him have been grofly deceived. Whether they have been in error will be for you to judge, when you have heard the evidence that fhall be ad-duced

The crime imputed to the prifoner ftands in the firft rank of the catalogue of thofe offences which our laws punifh with the utmoft feverity. The crime imputed is that of wilful and delibe-rate murder. An offence which, from being a *Felony* at common law, the Legiflature thought expedient in this kingdom to conftitute *High Treafon*

The circumftances of this unhappy tranfaction are fhortly thefe The late Mr George Rey-nolds thought, upon what grounds I need not mention, that he had received fome injury from Mr Keon, for which he was intitled to redrefs. In confequence of that opinion, he fent a mef-fage

fage to Mr Keon to meet him according to thofe rules of honor to which *our* laws give no fanction ——Whatever advantage the prifoner can have from this circumftance, that the meffage was fent by Mr. Reynolds, he is entitled to avail himfelf of it. That meffage was delivered by Mr Plunket, and it was agreed between him, Mr Keon, and his friend, that the piftols fhould only be charged with powder, to which mode, it will appear to you, that Mr Keon entirely acceded, and it was fettled by all the parties on the evening preceding the day of meeting, that powder only fhould be made ufe of on that occafion Singular as it may feem, it will be clearly proved, that the two principals, and their friends, knew that no balls were to be brought to the field on the day of meeting It is obvious that the only object of this meeting was to preferve the apppearance of adhering to thofe maxims of Honor, which it was conceived on that occafion to be neceffary to obferve, but that on the part of Mr Reynolds, or of his friend who attended him, there was no idea entertained of doing or attempting an injury to any perfon

On the faith of this agreement Mr. Reynolds, attended by Mr Plunket, came to the place appointed on the morning of the 16th October, 1786, and Mr. Reynolds, alighting from his horfe, advanced to Mr Keon, who was on the ground before him, and was attended by three or four o her perfons Mr Reynolds had in his hand a flight whip, and on coming up to Mr Keon, he took off his hat, and bid Mr. Keon, Good morning, who immediately replied, " Damn you, you fcoundrel, why did you bring me here?" and prefenting a piftol, which he held in his hand,

clofe

Rex
re fus
Keo.

clofe to his forehead, directly fired at Mr Reynolds, and fhot him through the head. He inftantly fell and expired. Mr Plunket was, for his own fafety, obliged to ride off the ground with all poffible expedition.

Thefe are the fingular circumftances of the fact you are to try, and let me afk, to what motive in the breaft of the prifoner can we afcribe this deed? Is it to the heat of paffion, which the law, in tendernefs to human frailty, will fometimes allow as an extenuation?—He had the whole preceding night to compofe his mind, and determine his conduct for the morning. Is it to be afcribed to fear for his own life?—That life, he knew, was in fafety by the previous agreement that had been made. Can we then attribute his actions on that day to any other motive in the human mind, but to that deep and fettled malice which conftitutes the act—deliberate murder?

Yet let it be in your remembrance, Gentlemen of the Jury, that the more atrocious the crime impeached, the clearer ought to be the proof. Every man is, by law, prefumed to be innocent, 'till he is proved to be guilty; and the deeper the guilt that is charged upon any man, the greater fhould be your caution in lending your belief to the charge. Sift, therefore, the evidence that fhall be produced to you in fupport of the profecution, confider the character of the witneffes, weigh the confiftency of their teftimony, and if, on any of thefe grounds, you find juft reafon to doubt of the truth of the accufation againft the prifoner at the bar, never vift upon him your indignation againft the offence; but bring in, without hefitation, a verdict of acquittal. Should you, on the other hand,

fee

see no reasonable grounds to doubt upon the evidence of the guilt that is imputed to him, let no weak motive of mistaken lenity lead you to forget what you owe to the community and to your oaths, but discharge your duty with the firmness that becomes men, to whom the Crown and the Prisoner have appealed on this solemn occasion.

It is matter of real satisfaction to those concerned for the prosecution to observe, that the prisoner comes upon his trial with every possible advantage which an accused man could desire. A long period has elapsed between the accusation and the trial, the prisoner has had ample time to prepare himself for his defence, and it cannot be presumed but that all proper exertions have been made during that interval, to lay his case before you in the most favourable light — A respectable Jury, composed of gentlemen, to not one of whom the prisoner has himself any objection, is impanelled to try him, the Counsel instructed to defend him are in the first rank of their profession, and last of all, he has the united wisdom of this Court, whom the humanity of the law makes counsel for the prisoner, to guard him against any illegal proceedings.— Thus sheltered and protected, he has nothing to fear, if he is innocent, and it is for you to say, whether he should have any thing to hope, if he be guilty.

First

Firſt Witneſs, JAMES PLUNKETT, Eſq;

Examined by Mr. CALDBECK.

Q. Did you know George Nugent Reynolds?
A. I did.
Q. Is he living or dead?
A. He is dead.
Q. Do you know the cauſe of his death?
A. I do
Q. What was it?
A. He was ſhot by Mr. Robert Keon.
Q. When did this happen?
A. On Monday the 16th of October, 1786.
Q. Do you remember any thing that happened previous to the meeting between Mr. Reynolds and Mr Keon, and tell the whole of the tranſaction?
A. I ſaw Mr. Keon the night before at his own houſe, or his brother's, I do not know which. I had gone to it by the deſire of Mr. Reynolds. I had a converſation with Mr Keon, about the buſineſs Mr Reynolds had ſent me about, I had met Mr Robert Keon and his brother at the door, and they aſked me in. They had been drinking punch, and after a few glaſſes, I ſaid, I was very ſorry that any difference had taken place between Mr Robert Keon and Mr. Reynolds, and that I wiſhed to accommodate the difference.
Q. What was the anſwer to that?
A. All the Mr Keons ſaid that Mr. Reynolds had uſed them ſo ill, and particularly their brother Robert, by letters written to him, that it was impoſſible.—There was one of the brothers

thers, Mr. Edward Keon, ſeemed more inclined to ſettle than the reſt.

Q What did you do in conſequence thereof?

A. Finding them all oppoſing a ſettlement, I called Mr. Edward Keon into an oppoſite parlour, and begged his aſſiſtance to ſettle the affair. —He ſaid it would be impoſſible, conſidering the ill uſage that Ambroſe Keon had received.—I preſſed Edward ſtrongly, and he wiſhed he ſaid any means could be contrived to ſettle the affair, and he would join me with all his heart in it.

Q. Did you propoſe any means?

A. I did.

Q. What were they?

A. I propoſed to him, that as I was to be friend to Mr. Reynolds, he ſhould be friend to his brother, that we ſhould contrive to charge the piſtols with powder A ſhot might paſs between them, and the public ſhould know nothing of this, and the affair might thus be ſettled

Q Was there any further converſation about this buſineſs?

A. Yes. After this was agreed upon we returned to the room, where we left the reſt drinking —After a ſhort ſpace of time, for fear of any miſtake, I called out Mr. Ned Keon again, to remind him of our agreement. I aſked him if he had a perfect recollection of it; he ſaid he had, and the whole of the agreement was again repeated.

Q. Do you know who repeated it?

A I cannot tell whether it was repeated by Mr. Edward Keon or myſelf; but I am ſure it was repeated by one of us.

Q. Did the priſoner know any thing of this agreement?

A. He did

Q How

Q. How do you know that?

A. I, shortly after my return with Mr Edward Keon, went to the door of the house, accompanied by Mr. Edward Keon, and Mr Robert Keon with him — thereupon told him that we had settled it in such a manner, as that nothing could happen to either of them, as they were both to fire with powder.

Q. What did the prisoner say?

A. He at first objected, and refused to comply, but he afterwards said to me "*do as you p'ease*"

Q. When did you next see Mr Keon?

A. About eight o'clock in the morning

Q. Had you had any communication with the deceased previous to meeting Mr Keon next?

A. I had

Q. What was it?

A. I acquainted him with the agreement.

Q. What impression did you wish to make on the deceased's mind thereby?

A. I wished to impress him with an idea that Robert Keon was convinced that no injury could be sustained by the meeting.

Q. Did Mr Reynolds give any directions to you, and what were they?

A. He desired me to be careful to charge the pistols myself with powder, and not to trust it to them

Q. Whom did he mean by them?

A. He meant either Robert or Edward Keon.

Q. Where did you go the next morning?

A. To the place appointed.

Q. In whose company?

A. In the company of Mr Reynolds.

Q. What had you in your hands?

A. We had each of us a small whip.

Q. Who

Rex
verſus
Keon.

Q. Who befides were with you?

A. Mr Reynold's fervant and mine.

Q. From the Court —How many piftols were there between you and Mr Reynolds?

A. One cafe between us, which my fervant carried unloaded

Q Where were you to meet Mr. Keon?

A. I thought it had been on the hill of Shee-more, but I found them at the top of a hill about a mile from the place which I apprehend-ed to have been the place appointed

Q Did you fee the prifoner there?

A I did, and——

Q You need not mention any other as they are not now on their trials —What did you then do?

A. I leaped into where I faw them in the fields.

Q What did Mr. Reynolds do?

A He followed me on foot.

Q Were you or Reynolds armed?

A. No. We were both unarmed.

Q In what fituation was Mr. Keon?

A. I *believe all* the Keons were on foot, and I know that Mr. Robert Keon was on foot and Mullirky, but I cannot pofitively fay, whether the reft were on foot or not

Q Was Mr Robert Keon armed?

A. He was —He had a piftol in each hand, Mr. Edward Keon had a cafe of piftols, and Mr. Ambrofe Keon had a cafe of piftols

Q. Had they any other weapons?

A I cannot fay whether they had any other weapon or not.

Q Had Mr Reynolds any weapon?

A I am certain he had no weapon but a fmall whip, unlefs he had it concealed.

Q Could

Q. Could he have any concealed weapon un-
known to you?

A. I am fure he had no concealed weapon.

Q Had you any weapon?

A None but a whip

Q. Did any thing pafs between you and Mr.
Robert Keon?

A. Yes

Q What was it?

A I fpoke to Mr. Robert Keon, and begged
he would behave politely to Mr Reynolds, as I
had inftructed Mr Reynolds to do fo to him.

Q What anfwer did Mr Keon give you?

A. He faid he would act as he ought.

Q What followed this?

A Mr Robert Keon went up towards Mr.
Reynolds, and I rode forward to Mr Edward
Keon, feeing fuch a preparation, to afk him the
reafon for it, and to learn if any change had
taken place I heard Mr Reynolds fay, " Good
morrow, Mr. Keon," and I heard Mr Robert
Keon fay fomething in return, and I think it
began with either the word *rafcal* or *fcoundrel*,
but I cannot pofitively fay whether the fhot or
the expreffion made me turn about, but when I
turned, I faw Mr Reynolds with his hand to his
hat, either lifting it from, or to his head, the
blood gufhing from his head, and he inftantly
falling

Q Did you fee Mr. Reynolds fall?

A I did

Q. Did his hat fall in his hand?

A I cannot tell whether it did or not?

Q In what fituation was Mr. Robert Keon?

A He was inclined forward, his hand ftretch-
ed forward, and a piftol in it

Q. Did you fee any fmoke?

A. I

A I cannot recollect, whether I did or not.

Q In what direction was Mr. Keon's hand?

A Towards Mr Reynolds

Q What distance was Mr Keon from Mr Reynolds?

A As they stood from me it appeared to be about two or three yards, but I understood from others it was nearer?

Q Was there any other person near Mr Keon besides Mr Reynolds?

A Yes, my servant was so near, that if he missed Mr Reynolds he must (as I believe) have killed either the horse which my servant rode, or my servant

Q What is that servant's name?

A. Luke Ternan.

Q Did Mr Reynolds do any thing after this?

A. No   He never moved or spoke after this, as I understood — My mare had started at the report of the shot, and I lost my reins, but I never saw Mr Reynolds stir or speak after

Q Did you see Mr Reynolds after, so as to see where he was wounded?

A Yes   The wound was over the eye, and the ball was extracted at the back of his head

Q Did you do any thing in consequence of all this?

A I exclaimed, " You have murdered the gentleman, you villain," or somewhat of horror, at the act

Q. What happened thereon?

A My servant struck at my horse, and bid me ride away as fast as I could, else I should be murdered

Q Did you take his advice?

A I did   But as I was getting away, I saw Mr. Ambrose Keon with a pistol in each hand, and a man galloping after me. I called to my

servant

Rex
versus
Keon,

ſervant for one of my piſtols, and he told me
they could be of no uſe to me, as they were not
charged I took one of my piſtols from him,
and then the man who rode after me deſiſted
from his purſuit, and rode back

Croſs-examined by the PRIME SERJEANT.

Q What is the practice, Mr Plunket, on theſe
occaſions as to charging the piſtols?

A. I apprehend that it is uſual to charge them
on the ground

Q Was there not an agreement that Mr. Keon
was to be aſſaulted?

A No, there was no ſuch agreement.

Q Did you not hear of, or inſiſt upon it, that
Mr Reynolds muſt ſtrike Mr Keon?

A. I never did hear or inſiſt upon ſuch a
thing

Q Were you a ſpectator of what had happened in the intermediate time after you had
paſſed Mr. Keon?

A. No, ſave hearing the ſhot or word

Q. How much farther on was Mr. Edward
Keon?

A He was about fifteen yards farther on than
Mr. Robert Keon

Q In what ſituation were Mr Keon and Mr.
Reynolds with regard to you?

A. Mr Robert Keon was nearer to me than
Mr. Reynolds, and Mr Keon had his back towards me.

Q Did you, or did you not, deliver Mr Robert
Keon a meſſage?

A I do not recollect that I delivered Mr.
Robert Keon poſitively a meſſage.

Q. Do

Q. Do you recollect the situation of the ground where Mr Keon and Mr. Reynolds met?

A I do The spot where Mr Keon was, was rather a rising ground, and the spot where Mr. Reynolds was shot, was a hollow, when Mr Reynolds was shot, Mr Keon was over him

Q Where was Mr Reynolds's servant?

A He remained with his master's horse, as I believe, outside the field.

Q How far had Mr Reynolds came into the field?

A Not above three or four yards.

Q Did not Mr Reynolds's servant come into the field

A Not to my knowledge I believe he remained outside of the wall, and if he came into the field, I did not see him

Q How come your pistols to be uncharged?

A When I came out I expected no serious business was to be done.

Q. Had you no balls about you?

A. Yes, I had put a brace of balls in my waistcoat pocket when I left my own house, in consequence of having received a letter from Mr. Reynolds, requesting me to deliver a message.

Q. Were not your pistols charged?

A Yes, after Mr Reynolds was shot, I charged one of them in my own defence.

Q With whom was the agreement made that you have so frequently mentioned?

A. With Mr Edward Keon.

Q. Did not Mr Robert Keon say that he would not consent to it?

A. Yes, at first—but he afterwards said, "Do as you please."

Q Can

Q. Can you positively take upon you to say Mr Reynolds did not strike him?

A. I cannot.

Second Witness, PATRICK BRENAN.

Examined by Mr CURRAN.

Q Did you know George Nugent Reynolds?

A I did—I was his servant.

Q Is he living or dead?

A He is dead.

Q When did he die?

A. He died on the 16th of October, last year.

Q How do you know he is dead?

A I saw him dead—he was shot by Mr Robert Keon

Q How do you know that?

A. I was in Mr. Reynolds's service at that time, and went that morning in company with my master, along with Mr. Plunket and his servant, to a place called Drynaun

Q How were you armed?

A My master, nor I, nor Mr Plunket, had any arms, only one case of pistols, which were with Mr Plunket's servant.

Q. What did you see when you came to Drynaun?

A I saw five persons, Michael Mullarky, Patrick Carty, and the three Mr Keons.

Q Did you know them before?

A I did

Q. Did you know Robert Keon?

A I did

Q Had they, or which of them, any arms?

A The three brothers, Robert, Ambrose, and Edward were armed, Robert had a case of pistols

Q Where

Q. Where had Robert the piftols?

A. I believe he had them in his pocket before he came up to my mafter, but I faw them in his hand when he came up to my mafter.

Q. In what fituation were the Keons when you firft faw them?

A. They were ftanding together when I firft faw them, as if confulting.

Q. When you firft faw them, what did your mafter do?

A. He alighted on the road and gave his horfe and his coat to me, and then went over the wall, and went forward about two or three yards.

Q. What happened then?

A. Robert Keon advanced towards him.

Q. How was your mafter armed?

A. He had no arms, only a flight cutting whip? *

Q. Defcribe your mafter's conduct to Mr. Keon?

A. My mafter took off his hat with one hand, and held down the whip in the other.

Q. Did he fay any thing?

A. Good morrow to you, Mr Keon.

Q. Did Mr Keon fay or do any thing in confequence of this, and what?

A. Mr. Keon faid, "Damn you, you fcoundrel, what bufinefs had you with me here," and before he had thefe words well out of his mouth, he fhot my mafter.

Q. Take care and confider of what you are faying,—are you certain you faw every thing that you now relate? Confider that the life of the prifoner at the bar depends on it

A. I had my eye upon every thing, and faw every thing, for I had Robert Keon and my mafter conftantly in my view

* Here he fhewed the whip which his mafter had, and the hat which he wore

Q At

Q At what diftance were you from Mr Keon and Mr Reynolds when this happened ?

A I was at the diftance of feven or eight yards, under or over

Q What diftance were Mr. Keon and Mr. Reynolds afunder when the fhot took place ?

A They were fo near, that I cannot tell whether Mr Keon laid the piftol on Mr Reynolds's head or not.

Q Was Mr Keon fo near that he could have reached Mr. Reynolds with the piftol ?

A He was.

Q Did you fee any thing more ?

A Yes, I faw my mafter drop

Q Defcribe the pofition, if you can, in which he dropped ?

A. He fell the moment he received the fhot, in the pofture of faluting Mr Keon.

Q. In what fituation was his whip ?

A. He had it in the other hand hanging down.

Q. Did he ftrike at Mr Keon ?

A He never made any attempt to ftrike Mr. Keon *

He was crofs examined by Mr. RECORDER.

Q To whom did you firft give an account of this tranfaction ?

A To my miftrefs

Q Are you certain you gave no account of it on the road, before you returned to your miftrefs ?

A. I am certain that as I came home I was crying and roaring that my mafter was dead.

* He was afked three or four other queftions, but as they feem to relate to other perfons, who may hereafter be tried, they are omitted

Q. In what fituation did you ftand to the deceafed and the prifoner Mr Keon?

A. I ftood very convenient to them on the road.

Q I mean, were their faces, or their fides, or their backs, towards the road?

A Some had their faces to the road, and fome not.

Q. Where did your mafter alight?

A. He alighted on the road.

Q Was there a high wall between the place where Mr. Reynolds and Mr Keon met and the road?

A. Part of the wall was high, and part of it low.

Q. Did not you alight to hold your mafter's ftirrup?

A. I did not.

Q Why did you not?

A. Becaufe he did not require it.

Q. In what fituation was your mafter as to you, when he went into the field? I mean, was his face or his back to you?

A. His back was to me.

Q. Did he not run into the field in a great hurry and paffion?

A. No, he was going on fair and eafy

Q. How did your mafter ftand as to you and Mr Keon—I mean, was Mr. Keon between you and your mafter, or how otherwife?

A My mafter ftood directly between me and Mr. Keon

Q. Would you not have been in danger yourfelf, if you had ftood in the fame line with your mafter?

A. Perhaps I was not in the particular line, or elfe I fhould have been in danger.

G   Q Which

Q. Which were you or Mr. Plunket's servant nearest to Mr. Keon ?

A. Mr Plunket's servant was nearest.

Q. How was Plunket's servant situated as to Mr. Reynolds ?

A. He was rather on one side of him.

Q. Were you at Mr Keon's house at any time after ?

A. Yes, I was at old Mr. Keon's house, their father's, that day.

Q. Who went with you there ?

A. A Mr. Johnson, and Mr. Cunningham, a Justice, came along with me

Q. Where had Mr. Keon the pistols when you first saw him ?

A. It must have been in his pocket that he had them.

Q. Who was the first person who examined you as to this business ?

A. The Coroner.

Q. How were you examined , I mean, were you upon oath ?

A. I was.

Q. Who next examined you ?

A. Mr Burchell, a magistrate.

Q. How did he examine you ?

A He examined me upon oath.

Q. Who else examined you ?

A. Mr Morton, another Justice of Peace, was by when Mr Burchell took the examinations, and he signed them.

Q. Who else examined you ?

A. I was examined before my Attorney and Lawyer before the Assizes.

Q. That was upon oath too ?

A. No, it was not.

Q. Do you write or read ?

A. No,

A. No, I can neither read or write

Q. Was there not some paper read to you in Dublin, that you had told before relative to this paper?

A. There was not.

Q. Did you not make an affidavit in Dublin?

A. I did, but not in this business.

Q. Were you not examined by your Attorney?

A. I gave my instructions to my Attorney, who took them down

Earlsfort, C. J ——Do you mean to throw any imputation, Mr. Recorder, on examining the witness previous to a trial ——I confess it appears to me to be a very honest industry, which tends to relieve Counsel, the Court and the Jury, of irrelevant and impertinent matter.

Here the Recorder closed his examination, and the Counsel for the Crown closed the Case; praying leave to rebut any new matter which might be suggested on the defence of the prisoner

The Prime Serjeant then urged that nothing appeared against the other four, but the Court over-ruled that assertion.

Rex versus Keon.

G 2   DEFENCE.

DEFENCE.

The first Witness for the Prisoner, LAWRENCE
SHANLY.

Examined by Mr. BLOSSET.

Q Do you remember the sixteenth of October, twelve-month?

A. I do

Q Where were you that morning?

A I was going to work to Mr William Keon's

Q Did you cross any fields?

A. I crossed many a field

Q. I mean, were you near Drynaun?

A I was near the lands of Drynaun.

Q Did you see any body there and whom?

A I saw five people there

Q Who were they?

A I saw Mr. Robert Keon, and Ambrose Keon, and Mr. Edward Keon, and Michael Mullarky, and Patrick Carty

Q. Did you see any body else there?

A. Yes, I saw Mr Reynolds there.

Q When did you see Mr Reynolds there?

A. As he was going into the field

Q Before he went into the field what did he do?

A I left his horse on the road, and threw his surtout coat to his servant.

Q When Mr Reynolds went into the field, was he on foot or on horseback?

A He was on foot.

Q What temper did he seem to be in?

A He seemed to be in a passion.

Q How did he get into the field?

A. He

A. He went over the wall into the field.

Q. Did he slip or stumble?

A. He did, and his hat came down over his face more than usual, and he lifted it up with his left hand

Q. Had Mr. Reynolds any thing in his other hand?

A. He had a whip in it.

Q. Did he do any thing with it?

A. Yes, he shook it two or three times at Robert Keon, as he advanced, and while he advanced he struck at him

Q. In what way had he his whip?

A. He clubed it

Q. Did he strike Mr. Keon more than once?

A. After he had clubed his whip, he struck at Mr Keon as fast as he could draw, and at the third stroke Mr Keon lifted his hand with the pistol in it, and Mr. Reynolds struck the pistol, and it went off

He was cross-examined by Mr. CALDBECK.

Q. Do you know John Reynolds?

A. No

Q. Did you ever hear of him?

A. Yes, very often.

Q. Do you know Patrick Brenan?

A. I do

Q. Where was he when you saw all that you have told a while ago?

A. He was going away to tie his master's horse that he had led away to a bush

Q. How far was he from what happened?

A. About twenty or thirty yards

Q. How far do you live from Drynaun?

A. About

A. About ſix or ſeven miles.

Q What brought you there then ?

A I was going to my work to ſaw timber.

Q Where were you at work ?

A. At Mr William Keon's, at Keon's-bridge.

Q How far were you from Mr Robert Keon, that you ſaw this ſo well ?

A So near that I could ſee every thing

Q Was there any wall between you and them ?

A There was a mearing between us, but I was on a height

Q Then you could ſee every thing that happened ?

A I could ſee a hare going the road

Q Was there any wall between Mr. Reynolds and you ?

A Yes, there was.

Q What kind of wall was it ?

A it was in ſome places high, and in others low.

Q What time was it when you were going to work ?

A Between ſix and eight o'clock in the morning

Q Do you uſually go to work ſo early ?

A I uſually go to work at ſix in the morning.

Q Do you know John Reynolds ?

A I know a great many John Reynolds's

Q Did you ſee that man, *(pointing to a man)* that morning ?

A I did not ſee him that morning

Q Were not you in his company that morning ?

A Not that I know of

Q Were you not in his company ?

A. If

A If I was, I do not know it.
Q What did you do when this affair ended ?
A I went to my work
Q Did you go no where elfe ?
A Yes, I went to Dennis Kelly's
Q Did you tell the fame ſtory there ?
A Yes, I did

Second *Witneſs*, PATRICK DONNELLY.

Examined by Mr. O'CONNOR.

[Donnelly being an Iriſh witneſs, an interpreter
was ſworn.]

Q Do you remember the 16th of October ?
A. I do.
Q. Did you ſee Robert Keon that day ?
A. I did.
Q. Do you remember what paſſed ?
A. I ſaw the three Keons, Mullarky and
Carty.
Q Did you ſee Mr. Reynolds ?
A. I did, and his friend, and their ſervants.
Q. Did you ſee any ſtrokes ?
A. Yes, George Reynolds ſtruck two blows
at Robert Keon, and on making a third blow his
piſtol went off, and Reynolds fell

He was croſs-examined by Mr. CURRAN.

Q Do you know the laſt witneſs, Laurence
Shanly ?
A. No ; but I know Laurence Shanly, a faw-
yer.

Q Did

Q Did you see him that morning ?

A. Yes

Q Where did you see him ?

A Inside the lands of Drynaun.

Q. What was Shanly doing ?

A He was going backward and forward.

Q How was he dreſſed ?

A He had a brown wrapper on.

Q. How near was Shanly to you?

A. He was a ſpace from me.

Q What do you mean by a ſpace, how many yards ?

A. I do not know

Q. Was he twenty, or thirty, or forty yards from you ?

A. I believe he was forty yards from me

Q. What kind of hat did Mr Reynolds wear ?

A. He had three cocks in his hat

Q. Do you know James Murphy ?

A. I do.

He was examined by Lord Earlsfort.

Q Do you know whether Shanly could ſee you as well as you ſaw him ?

A. I cannot tell.

Q Where did you see Shanly firſt that day ?

A. I did not ſee him until this affair was over

Third Witneſs, Christopher Dillon.

Examined by Mr Smith.

Q. Did you know George Nugent Reynolds ?

A. I did

Q When did you ſee him laſt ?

A. At

A At laſt Summer Aſſizes, at Carrick-on-Shannon, and not ſince.

Q Had you any converſation with him about Mr Robert Keon?

A None that I remember

Q What buſineſs had you with Mr. Reynolds?

A I was the hair-dreſſer who dreſſed him

Q Did he declare any thing to you about Mr. Keon?

A Not that I recollect

Q Did you not yourſelf ſay, before this, that Mr. Reynolds had made ſome declarations about Mr. Keon?

A I do not know but I did

[This witneſs was not croſs-examined]

Fourth Witneſs, FRANCIS MORAN

Examined by Mr STANLEY

Q Do you know the priſoner?

A I do

Q Did you ſee him at Drynaun?

A I did.

Q. When did you ſee him?

A. At about ſeven or eight o'clock in the morning.

Q Whom did you ſee there firſt?

A. I ſaw Mr Robert Keon

Q When did you ſee Mr Reynolds firſt?

A As ſoon as he came to the hill of Drynaun.

Q. What did Mr Reynolds then do?

A He alighted from his horſe, took off his coat, and went acroſs the wall, in his going

H

over the wall, his hat fell down on his face, and he lifted it up

Q Had Mr. Reynolds any thing in his hand ?

A Yes; he had a light whip.

Q Did Mr. Reynolds ſay or do any thing to Mr. Keon?

A He ſhook his whip at him two or three times, and ſtruck him twice acroſs the head.

Q Where were you when this happened ?

A I was on the ſide of the hill

Q. How was Mr Reynolds wounded?

A I ſuppoſe Mr Keon fired the ſhot, after being ſtruck

Q Did you ſee Brenan ?

A. Yes, I did

Q Was he on foot, or on horſeback ?

A He was on foot

Q Could he ſee Mr Reynolds and Mr. Keon as well as you?

A He could not.

Q Why ſo ?

A Becauſe he went into a hollow, and I was on the ſide of a hill

He was croſs-examined by Mr Duqurry.

Q How do you think Mr. Reynolds was ſhot ?

A I ſuppoſe the piſtol in Mr. Keon's hand ſhot him.

Q How many ſtrokes did Mr. Reynolds give Mr Keon ?

A. Two ſtrokes on the head, and one on the hand and piſtol

Q How ſoon after this ſtroke on the hand did Mr. Keon's piſtol go off ?

A The whip was ſcarcely off the piſtol before it went off.

Q Did

Q Did you hear what paſſed between Mr. Keon and Mr Reynolds?

A No, I did not.

Q What did Mr Reynolds firſt do when he came into the field where Mr Keon was?

A The firſt thing he did was to ſhake his whip at him

Q How near was Mr Reynolds to Mr Keon when he ſhook the whip?

A About three or four yards from him

Q Did he do any thing elſe with his whip, beſides ſhaking it at Mr Keon?

A. Yes, he turned it in his hand, and ſtruck him.

Q Pray what weapons had Mr Keon?

A He had two piſtols in his hand

Q Are you ſure that it was out of Mr Keon's piſtol the ſhot came that killed Mr Reynolds?

A Yes, I am ſure it was out of Mr. Keon's piſtol it came

Q Pray did you ſee any body follow Mr. Plunket?

A No, I did not

Examined by LORD EARLSFORT

Q. Do you know Patrick Donnelly?
A I do
Q Do you know Laurence Shanly?
A I do
Q How long do you know them?
A I have known them both many years
Q Did you ſee them at Drynaun that day?
A. I did
Q Did they ſee you?
A They might have ſeen me.

Q When

Q When did you fee them laft?

A We came up to town together.

Q. Did you know what teftimony they were to give?

A Not till we came to town

Q Did they know what evidence you were to give?

A I believe they did

Q Why do you believe fo?

A Becaufe I told it to them

Q Do you remember the affizes of Carrick?

A I do

Q Do you remember the trial that was to have been then?

A I do

Q Did you know what they had to fay then -

A No

Q Did they know what you had to fay?

A No

Q When had you firft any converfation with them about your teftimony?

A Never until I came to Dublin

Fifth Witnefs, MYLES KEON, Efq;

Examined by Mr. KING.

Q Did you know the late Mr Reynolds?

A. I did very well.

Q When did you fee him laft before his death?

A I faw him in the month of October 1786, at his own houfe, two days before this unhappy accident

Q Did you ever hear him fay any thing about Robert Keon?

A. I

A I have often heard him threaten to ill use Robert Keon.

Q Did you ever hear him use any particular threat against him?

A I heard him say that he would horse-whip him wherever he met him.

He was cross-examined by Mr CURRAN.

Q Are you any relation to the prisoner?

A I am

Q What relation are you to him?

A A very remote one

Q Pray in what degree?

A. Robin Keon's great-grandfather was uncle to my grandfather

Q When did you hear Reynolds threaten to horse-whip Keon?

A In more than one place, but as I best recollect, Mr Reynolds shewed me, at his house, a letter in which he promised to meet Robin Keon on Sunday

Q What was the cause of this quarrel?

A Several letters which had passed between them, and in particular a letter which the deceased had written to his mother

Q Did you not understand that letter to be a general dissuasion from using Mr. Keon as her agent?

A. I did not

Q What was your reason for not believing it to be so?

A He, in the letter, described Robert Keon as a Brecknock, and said that the agent was worthy of the client, and the client worthy of the agent.

Q. Did

Q Did you not hear, and do you not believe, that Keon ftruck Mr. Reynolds in an affize town, and at an affizes?

A I have heard and believe he did

Q Well, Sir, and did Mr. Reynolds make a manly refiftance?

A I believe he did not

Q Come Sir, the man is gone, and his valour does not now fignify, do you believe that he was a man of courage?

A I believe he was not, becaufe he declared it himfelf

Q Have you not heard that he was often beaten, and bore it with patient and becoming meeknefs?

A. He never was beaten to my knowledge, except by Colonel St. George, and this once by Mr. Keon

Q Was Mr. Keon armed with piftols the time he ftruck Mr Reynolds in Carrick?

A. He was not.

Q What hindered him from beating Mr Reynolds more feverely than he did?

A Two other Mr. Keons interpofed.

Sixth Witnefs, WILLIAM KEON.

Examined by Mr. WHITESTONE.

Q What relation are you to Mr. Robert Keon?

A. I am his brother.

Q Do you remember the 15th of October. 1786?

A I do.

Q Did

Q Did you ſee Mr. Plunket any where that day?

A. I did, at my father's houſe

Q Did he ſpeak any thing about what brought him there?

A He ſaid he came to bring about a meeting between my brother and Mr. Reynolds, and expreſſed great concern on account of the buſineſs which he came about, and declared that he would not have come had it not been on account of Mr. Reynolds, his own relation.

Q Did you know the late George Reynolds?

A I knew both him and his father

Q Did you ever hear George Reynolds ſay any thing about your brother?

A Yes, he told me that he muſt bring my brother to an account for his aſſaulting him, and that he was adviſed, by his friend Mr Plunket, that he ought not to meet him until he had ſtruck him, and that his wife would not ſleep with him until he had met Robin Keon.

The Counſel on behalf of the Crown declined croſs-examining Mr. William Keon, and the defence being cloſed, the Counſel for the Proſecution propoſed to examine a witneſs to rebut the teſtimony of Laurence Shanly; and accordingly called

JOHN REYNOLDS—*who was examined by* Mr
CURRAN.

Q. Do you know Laurence Shanly?
A. I do
Q. Where does he live?
A. He lives in Killyfad.

Q De

Q. Do you know the hill of Sheemore·

A. I do.

Q Do you recollect the day of Mr. Reynolds's death ?

A I do

Q. How far is Drynaun from where Shanly lives ?

A. Shanly then lived in Gurtneen, about feven or eight miles from Drynaun

Q. Did you fee Shanly on the day of Mr. Reynolds's death ?

A. I did

Q. Where did you fee him ?

A In his own houfe at breakfaft.

Q. At what time ?

A. At between eight and nine in the morning. I went to his houfe to get a fpade of mine to dig potatoes

Q When did you part from Shanly.

A. After getting my fpade, I left the houfe, and Shanly fet off for Mr William Keon's, where he was going to work

Q. When did you fee him next ?

A I faw him next day Having heard an account of the affair, I went from curiofity to learn the circumftances from him at his return

Q What did he tell you about the death of Mr. Reynolds ?

A He told me he had not been there until two hours after Mr Reynold's death , and that he heard of the accident at Drumfna.

Q. How far is Drumfna from where the acci dent happened ?

A It is about four or five miles.

Crofs-

Croſs-examined by the RECORDER.

Q What buſineſs are you?
A. A labourer
Q Do you know Mr Francis Waldron?
A. I do
Q. To whom do you pay your rent?
A To Mrs. Niſbitt
Q Who gave you the money to bring you
up?
A. I got no money but from Mr. Thomas
Niſbitt
Q Who did you tell this ſtory to firſt?
A. I told it firſt to Mr. Niſbitt.
Q. Why did you tell it?
A Becauſe he knew the fellow was not there.

The Counſel for the priſoner then tendered
evidence to prove that this laſt was not a credible witneſs, and for that purpoſe produced

Mr. FRANCIS WALDRON

Examined by Mr STANLEY.

Q. Do you know John Reynolds.
A I do
Q Do you believe he is a man to be credited
on his oath.
A. I do not believe he is to be credited on his
oath.

He was croſs-examined by Mr. CURRAN.

Q What induces you to believe him not to
be credited on his oath?

I

A. Becauſe

A Becaufe I heard him forfwear himfelf on the table, he faid he paid his rent to Mrs Nif-bitt. Now I am her agent, and I know he never did pay her any rent

Q. On whofe lands did Reynolds live, was it on the eflate of Mrs Nifbitt?

A Yes, it was but the land was fet to another tenant, under whom he held

Q. And becaufe an ignorant fellow miftook his landlord, you think him not to be believed on his oath?

A. I think he did not fwear the truth on the table

Q. Then before you heard him on the table in the morning, you would have thought him credible, tho' now you would not?

A I have other reafons to think he ought not to be credited, his mother is a poor widow, and his brother and he often let her want, and he ufed to drink

Q Then, Sir, becaufe the man miftook the perfon he paid rent to, and ill ufed his mother, you think he is not to be believed?—You may go down.

The cafe being here clofed, the *Prime Serjeant* obferved, that it was no part of his duty to fpeak to evidence, or to flate any cafe, but as it ftruck him the prifoner could not be found guilty of *murder*, and the utmoft ftretch to which the law would warrant the Jury to go, would be to convict him of *manflaughter*, if the Court were of opinion that the evidence went farther, he would hope to be heard.

Lord *Earlsfort*.—I think you ought not.—If there were any doubt, we would call on a Counfel

Rex *verfus* Keon.

fel or two. But I think there is not a point for ingenuity or stupidity to make. If a cafe had been ftated by the profecutor's Counfel to provoke the feelings of the auditors, I fhould have interrupted the gentleman who made it, and I confefs I wifh to remember every word of it, as the calmeft charge I could make to the Jury

CHARGE

Lord Earlsfort, Chief Juftice.

Gentlemen of the Jury,

UPON an occafion of this kind, I fhall make as few obfervations as poffible and thofe obfervations which I fhall make fhall not be to lead you, but merely for the purpofe of bringing forward in your mind the clear fubftance of every thing which admits of no doubt —There can be no doubt but that Reynolds was killed, there can be no doubt but he fell by a fhot from the prifoner and there can be no doubt, but this meeting was in confequence of a deliberate appointment There is a difference between the teftimony of Mr William Keon and that of Mr Plunket —If you believe Mr Plunket there was to be no duel, but a mock one, on the contrary, Keon feems to fay, his purpofe was to bring them out to a duel, but Plunket fwears exprefsly otherwife— There were no bullet to be put in, and the piftols were to be charged with powder only—Plunket had not put the piftols into Reynolds's hands, but they remained in the hands of Plunket's fervant. On the other hand, there were three cafes of piftols in the hands of the

I 2   Keons,

Keons, one of which was certainly loaded —If may be said that there can be no other evidence, becaufe all of the Keons are indicted except William —As to the agreement, if the prifoner was fatisfied to have no ball, it was a work of fhocking bafenefs, if not, he was determined effectually to fight a duel, and our law confiders a death in fuch a purfuit to be MURDER If you believe that feveral blows were ftruck by Reynolds at the prifoner, and one of thefe blows ftruck the piftol, and it went off by accident, you ought to acquit him · It is a queftion for you, gentlemen, to determine, whether it is probable that Reynolds would make three adverfe ftrokes againft a man armed with piftols, and feeing his two brothers armed in a like manner —you are the judges of probability But if you believe there was this agreement between the parties, which Plunket has fworn to, then Robert fired foully upon the deceafed, and it was murder, and a bafe and barbarous one. But my opinion goes farther—if one in a deliberate manner goes to fight a duel, and he falls, it is murder   Then if you believe he fired upon the deceafed difarmed, or not on equal terms, it is murder There has been a good defence fet up, if you believe it There were three ftrokes made at Robert, and the piftol went off. If you believe Robert did not intend to fhoot— when he ftood over the corpfe, after the deceafed fell, did he fhew any mark of contrition, repentance or remorfe? Duelling is only excufable, when a man retires back as far as he can, and then the law juftifies his drawing a fword or any other lethal weapon, but in this cafe Reynolds had no weapon of danger, and the only doubt that remains, is, if you can believe that

that the shot went off by the stroke, and in that case you must acquit the prisoner,—but if you cannot believe that, you must not trifle with your oaths but remember that humanity to an individual is cruelty to the multitude.—Your reasons for your belief, or disbelief, of any fact, must be the reasons of prudent men , and if your reason convinces you that the pistol went off by accident, I again tell you, you must acquit , but on the contrary, if you believe it to be an act of brutal wrath, after a good natured design of innocently satisfying mistaken honour, you must find the prisoner guilty

Smith, Counsel—Begged leave to account for the deceased's having struck the prisoner though armed, and urged that Reynolds knew that Keon's pistols were not charged

Lord Earlsfort ——See how that cuts—Reynolds believed the pistols not charged, and held himself in no danger , how will you understand the prisoner's answer to Plunket, " I will do as I ought."——What, on the contrary, was the language of Reynolds to Keon ? " Good-mor-" row to you "—And what the reply ? " You " scoundrel, why did you bring me here."—— Upon the whole, if you believe that Reynolds broke the peace, you will find the prisoner guilty of manslaughter only but there seems to be a very great degree of refinement in the distinctions to be made in that case

Henn, J ——Lord Earlsfort has been so full and able, both in his statement of facts, and

and in the law arifing from them, that I fhall not take upon me to add any thing to what he has ftated to you.

Bradftreet, J ——At this late hour I fhould feel myfelf culpable if I took up much of your time

I fhall only obferve to you, that there are different fpecies of HOMICIDE

If you believe the evidence on behalf of the Crown, you muft convict the prifoner of MUR-DER

But if you believe that two ftrokes were made by the deceafed at the prifoner, as the prifoner's witneffes inform you, however improper it might be for him to have had a loaded piftol in his hand, the killing the deceafed after fuch an attack, can be no more than MANSLAUGHTER at large

And if you believe the killing to be the effect of the ftroke upon the piftol, and that the piftol went off by accident, it can only be HOMICIDE *per infortunium*, and in that cafe, according to the beft modern decifions, you will acquit the prifoner generally

It is your province however to weigh the evidence, and the due credit to be given to the refpective witneffes, and let your confcience direct your verdict.

Bennett, J ——On behalf of the prifoner three witneffes were produced, Shanly, Donnelly, and Moran, if you credit them you muft take the whole of their teftimony together, and if you believe the third ftroke to have been given by the deceafed to the prifoner, you can find no verdict to affect his life.

The

The Jury retired from the box, and returned in about a quarter of an hour, with their verdict GUILTY.

Rex verfus Keon.

Mr. *Moore*, junior Counfel for the Crown, prayed judgment.

Bradftreet, J ——No, the prifoner muft have four days before judgment, to move in arreft of it, if he fhall be fo advifed.

The prifoner, Robert Keon, was remanded 'till further orders, and the feveral other prifoners were alfo remanded.

NOVEMBER 20, 1787. *B. R.*

By the Court.—Let Robert Keon be brought up on Thurfday next, to abide judgment.

NOVEMBER 21, 1787. *B. R.*

By the Court —Let Robert Keon be brought up on Monday next.

NOVEMBER 26, 1787. *B R.*

By the Court —Let Robert Keon be brought up on Wednefday the 28th of November.

NOVEMBER

Rex
verfus
Keon.

NOVEMBER 28, 1787—(the laft day of Term).

B. R.

The prifoner was brought up, puifuant to the above * order.

Earlsfort, C J —Is Robert Keon brought up ?

Gaoler.—He is

Earlsfort, C. J —Cleik of the Crown, read the indictment

The Clerk of the Crown read a docket from the indictment.

The *Prime Serjeent* —My Lords, the Crown has thought proper to grant me a licence to appear for the unhappy gentleman at your bar ; and if, as his Counfel, I fhall defire any thing which the Court thinks ought not to be granted, or with an impropriety which they ought to refift, I truft your Lordfhips will impute them to their true motive—a zeal which was dictated by honour, confcience, and duty to my client —I fhall therefore now humbly pray your Lordfhip, on behalf of the prifoner, that the *Certiorari*, the *Record* returned in confequence thereof, the *Habeas Corpus* and *Return* thereon, and the *Venire Facias* by which the Jury were fummoned, and the *Return* thereof, may be read.

---

* Thefe feveral delays were occafioned by the great trial of Newburgh and Burroughs, which was tried at the bar of this court, and took up a week.

No

No objection having been made at first to this motion, Lord Earlsfort observed that he was sorry to fee the cafe deferted, on which

Browne, G J of Counfel for the Crown, lamented that, in the abfence of his feniors, he was obliged to oppofe the Prime Serjeant whom he knew to be too well acquainted with the law to pretend that he had any right, to have any part of the proceedings whatfoever read, except the indictment, and he faid he founded himfelf in this affertion, from the authority of Layer's Cafe, which cafe he had endeavoured to look through fince he had heard it mentioned from the Bench, and it is there faid by Juftice Evre, " that the merit and juftice of the cafe depend " entirely upon the indictment, which muft be " read in order to underftand the true ftate of " the queftion, and to fee the facts to which " the witneffes are to be examined, it is there-" fore abfolutely neceffary that the indictment " fhould be read, but no one of thefe reafons " will ferve for reading the *venire*" And in the fame book, it is faid by Sir J Fortefcue Aland, a judge of as much legal learning as can be remembered on the King's Bench in Great Britain, " The Court will affift in *matters* of " law where they appear, but will never affift " the perfon with *facts* to make *points* of law," and again he fays, " I take it clearly there never " was a cafe where the proceedings of the Court " have been called for to be read to the prifo-" ner, and for no other purpofe but to make " *error* "——Supported by this authority, and fanctioned by the wifdom of fuch great men, on fo folemn an occafion, he did not doubt but he fhould have the opinion of the Court in his favour;

6 St. Tr 229

P 324.

P. 323.

K

vour;

Rex versis Keon

Court, and begged leave to remark, that this case had a particular recommendation to the attention of the Court, as it was determined so lately as the 9th of Geo. I. when criminal proceedings had taken a more favourable and constitutional aspect than they had formerly.

Bradstreet, J. asked the Prime Serjeant if he had any case to produce, to overthrow what Browne had said.

Foll. 47

The *Prime Serjeant* cited Murray of Broughton's Case, and asserted that Counsel were permitted to take extracts from the Record.

Bradstreet, J —That, as I remember, was a *collateral issue*, upon an act of parliament, sent into the Court of King's Bench by a *certiorari* out of Chancery.

Barr
ibid.

The *Prime Serjeant* then cited the Case of the King against Rogers and others.

Bradstreet, J —That also was a *collateral issue*, they were the men who had broken out of Maidstone gaol.

[supra]

Serjeant *Hewitt*, on the same side with the Prime Serjeant, cited Layer's case, to prove that the Counsel for the prisoner might suggest errors on the Record, and that the Court were bound to look into it, to see if the error suggested was to be found therein, and this, he said, was admitted by Serjeant Pengelly, who prosecuted Layer on behalf of the Crown.

Mr

Mr *Stanley* cited the Cafe of Charles Ratcliffe, Murray of Broughton's Cafe, Harvey's Cafe, and the Cafe of Rogers

Rex
ce fis
Keon
Furt 4c.
P. 5
5 51
b n 1010

Bradſtreet, J ——Theſe were all *collateral iſ-ſues*. The pirates were tried at *Maidſtone*.

The *Prime Serjeant* ——I am forry to make any oppoſition that will but tend to delay juſtice, but this being the laſt day of Term, I hope the Court will give time to conſider the ſeveral points which ſhall be ſuggeſted to the Court to make error, and which in my mind conſtitute the moſt nice and difficult errors, and though I do not ſpeak this with any confidence on my own part, yet I ſolemnly declare I feel no diffidence on the point, that I ſhall be able to ſhew the Court that there are errors, upon which they will be bound to *arreſt* the judgment.

Browne, G J roſe to reply, but was ſtopped by the Court.

Earlsfort, C J ——If there be error on the Record, the ſooner it is known the better, previous to the trial it was read upon motion of the priſoner's Counſel, not as a matter of right, I felt not a little that this cafe ſeemed to be deſerted by ſuperior Counſel This however gave an opportunity to gentlemen inferior in ſtation to manifeſt their induſtry, and I was glad they had thus ſhewed their attention and ſkill—— nor do I feel any heſitation to ſay, that if the gentlemen concerned in the proſecution had objected to the Record being read *in limine*, I ſhould have refuſed it If errors be ſtated and pointed out by the Counſel for the priſoner,

the

the Court will look into the Record, but if we find they are made merely to pick into the Record we shall resist them. Ordinary business must be done in the ordinary way. This is a question of very great consequence, and must take the lead of all others.

Bradstreet, J ——The Cases cited at the Bar, do not apply in these several places. The persons to whom the Records had been read, had been convicted in another place, and the Court could have had nothing to proceed upon if the Record were not read. When the proceedings were at first read, had it been demanded as a matter of right we should have resisted it. The prisoner has a right to have the Indictment read.

The Clerk of the Crown then read the Indictment slowly, and the Counsel for the prisoner took notes of it.

Mr *Prime Serjeant*—Since I am precluded by the opinion of the Court from having the several proceedings read, I must feel my way as well as I can, and with little preparation indeed, endeavour to point out such errors as I apprehend to be upon the Record, and the several proceedings. Thus circumstanced, I fear, I may suggest errors, which do not exist, and therefore I shall have reason to claim the indulgence of the Court, as it is more than probable I shall unfoundedly trespass upon their patience, but I address myself to a Court where mercy seasons justice, and where it is fitting that the unfortunate gentleman at the bar should know that he has hitherto experienced every indulgence which
the

the Court could, confiftent with their opinion, grant, that his evidence was liftened to with the patient humanity which dignifies the proceedings of a Court of Juftice, and he fhould love his Judges though he fhould lofe his caufe

The firft error I apprehend to be in the *Certiorari*, which in this cafe was the firft proceeding in this Court, and being iffued to remove an indictment from a foreign county into this Court, fhould, in my humble judgment, be made returnable on one of the known general returns of the Terms. By a Rule of the Court of King's Bench, ftated 1ft *Show* 336 it muft be returnable the firft return of the Term next after it iffued, whereas I apprehend it is made returnable either on Friday next after the morrow of the Holy Trinity, or on fome other day, which is not any one of the known general return days. I beg leave to ftate thofe returns, and to know if the *Certiorari* be made returnable on any of thofe days? or whether it be returned by thofe perfons to whom it is directed?

The next error which I fhall conjecture is, that the *Venire Facias*, iffued for the Jury, is not tefted on the day of the Return of the *Certiorari*; by which means there becomes a chafm in the proceedings

That the *Venire* was not made returnable on a general return day of the term, as by all the authorities it fhould be, when it iffues on an indictment removed by *Certiorari* from a foreign county. The *Venire* in the prefent cafe is returnable on Friday next after the morrow of Saint *Martin*, and your Lordfhips will find it laid down that "if the indictment be taken in "any other county than that wherein the King's Bench

Rex verfus Keon.

1ft Error.

N. B. Tit. Cert.

4 Black. Com. 26v.

2d Error.

3d Error.

2 Inft. 568

Rex
versus
Keon.

4 St Tr
778

Rex v
Roberts,
1 Wilson
77

" Bench fits, and is removed into the King's
" Bench, there ought to be fifteen days between
" the Tefte and Return '—and it muft be returnable on a known return day Your Lordships
will find the fame principle where a Traverfe to
an Inquifition comes into this Court from the
Court of Chancery. Upon this point the authorities are numerous and uniform, and no inftance
can be produced in the adminiftration of the
Criminal Juftice of Great Britain, wherein the
point was controverted or doubted

Though limitted my time for preparation was,
I did not come into Court unapprized of *Layer*'s
cafe, as cited by Mr Browne, its authority ftood
between me and *oyer* of the proceedings, but I
hope where it aniwers my purpofe, I fhall be
allowed the advantage of it *Layer* was firft
brought up to the bar, on the 31ft of October,
the *Habeas Corpus* was read on the motion of the
Counfel for the Crown On the 3d of November he was again brought up, there was then an
application and debate about fixing the day of
trial, whether it fhould be on the 19th, or whether the Court fhould give him further time On
which Lord Chief Juftice Pratt faid, " at this
" time there is no day for the Return but the
" Octave of Saint *Martin,* or the laft day of
" term " Here the Court looked only to the
known legal return day, and no other, and it
never once occurred to them to make a new
return day, nor can a Return be made in the
Crown Office, upon any but a known return
day If *Layer*'s cafe has made againft me in one
point, it is conclufive for me in this—I appeal
to the book,—let the book fpeak,—*Sit Liber*
judex. Here is the opinion of one Chief juftice
—What

—What was the opinion of Lord C J Holt in *Knightly's* cafe? Upon a queftion on what day the trial fhould be, Lord Holt fays, "that being on a *Certiorari*, the *Venire Facias* "muft be returnable on a general return day "There muft be fifteen days between the Tefte "and the Return" Upon the Attorney General's preffing for an earlier day, "No," fays the Chief Juftice, "it cannot be before Wednefday, "that is the Return day"

Rex *verfus* Keon.

1 St Tr 778

See the confequence—Here has been an erroneous *Venire*—and if judgment be given on a verdict by Jurors, appearing on a Procefs any way erroneous, the whole of the proceeding muft fall to the ground, becaufe the trial was wholly unwarranted, and confequently the iffue miftried

2 Hawk. 301 old edit 428 new edit

It is alfo for me to point out to your Lordfhips, that *Venire* was not for the trial of Robert Keon alone, but was a joint *Venire* for the trial of all the parties Upon a joint *Venire* only one pannel fhould be returned, but it appears by the Return, that the Sheriff returned feveral pannels, when he fhould only have returned one, and whether the pannel intended by the Sheriff be the one returned, or not, no man knows Here then clearly is a mif-return to the Writ, and where there is a mif return, it is fatal and cannot be cured, for even in civil cafes an error of this kind could not be cured before the ftatutes, and *a fortiori* could never be cured in criminal cafes, to which the ftatutes do not extend

4th Error.

5th Error.

2 Hawk. 302 old edit 429 new edit Cro Jac. 467 Am nd- nents & Jeof als.

In the next place, the *Venire* iffued before the party was in Court His firft appearance was on the 16th day of November, the day of his trial.

6th Error.

There

7th Error.

Rex
versus
Keon.

There is not any award of the *Venire* upon the Roll.

8th Error

The prisoner was never brought to the bar of this Court until the day of his trial. And all the proceedings previous to his trial, were had in his absence, and before the Court had any jurisdiction.

Sir *Samuel Bradstreet*, here mentioned his having committed the prisoner in the vacation

9th Error.

Mr *Prime Serjeant* — My Lords, it is with great deference I mention another objection, upon which it may be supposed this Court had given an opinion at the time of the trial —It appears upon the Return of the *Venire*, that three hundred and sixty persons were returned, and there is no instance in which a *Venire* has been returned into the Court of King's Bench from a foreign county of any such number, unless by the special direction of the Court.

Mr Justice *Bennet* mentioned *Layer's* case as against this doctrine.

Mr. *Prime Serjeant* replied, that *Layer's* was a case of High Treason, where he could challenge five and thirty.

Mr Justice *Bennett*.—So it was at common law in cases of felony. In *Layer's* case, one hundred and one were returned to try one person only; here there were five persons to be tried

Mr.

Lord *Earlsfort*, C.]—In the *King* aguinst *Sheehy*, in which I was Counsel, there were sixty returned.

Rex versus Keon

Mr. *Prime Serjeant*—If the profecutor can procure three hundred and fixty to be returned, it gives him a *veto* to every Juryman, and there is no poffibility of putting him to fhew caufe

Bennett, Juftice —This was over-ruled in *Layer's* cafe

6 St Tr

Mr. *Prime Serjeant*.—The prifoner and profecutor are by no means on an equality, which by law they ought to be, there was no cafe where the pannel was encreafed without the direction of the Court.

Court —Can the Court direct what is illegal?

Mr *Prime Serjeant* —I do not fay it would be illegal in the Court, but for any perfon to increafe the pannel without the direction of the Court, is what I contend to be illegal, oppreffive, and elufive of the ftatute of Edward The *Venire* was joint, and only one was tried, though the Record was made up againft all the five, and though they all ftood at the bar The profecutor had his election, and might have iffued a joint or feparate *Venire* Why were three hundred and fixty Jurors returned? Becaufe a joint trial was expected, and therefore the trial ought to have been joint, there is no inftance, no uncontradicted cafe can be produced in which this Court, fitting upon the trial of an

12 h Er ror

L

indictment

indictment removed from a foreign Court, fevered a pannel

Sir *Samuel Bradstreet,*]—Can you shew a case against it, where the Court refused to sever the pannel on application made? Is not this Court a Court of gaol delivery?

Mr *Prime Serjeant* —Yes, with respect to the proceedings in the county wherein they sit, but not in any other; nor can they proceed upon indictments removed from a foreign county, but regular process must issue, and there should be fifteen days between the Teste and the Return. If the process be joint, they have no power to sever the pannel returned, and to try the issue between the Crown and the Prisoner separately, but must try them all at one and the same time, and by the same Jury. It is true that Justices of gaol delivery, and the Court of King's Bench, sitting in that capacity, may sever the pannel, says *Hawkins,* I do not find that this can be done in any other Case, and therefore I am warranted to say it is not in the power of the Court to try several persons separately, when a joint *Venire* issues upon a joint indictment, a Juror challenged by one, must be drawn as to all For the purpose of separate trials, separate *Venires* issue against each, which would be needless if the Court could sever the pannels, and that was done in *Rookwood* and *Cranburne's*

4 St. Tr
660.

11th Error.
Case. Where a joint *Venire* has issued, there can be no severance, the trials must be joint, for they are all embarked in the same bottom. The trial in this Case was had on the very day of the Return, when it ought to have been on the *quarto die post,* it was had upon a day upon which

the

the Sheriff was not obliged to return the Jury, and when the Jurors were not amerciable, only two hundred and forty appeared, *non conftat*, but they all might have appeared on the right day, and I take it that the prifoner had a right to have the advantage of the whole Jury returned, fuch as it was. The prifoner could not legally be tried fooner, and his appearance does not *falve* the error.

The *Certiorari* defcribes the party with a different addition from that by which he is defcribed in the indictment, and I beg leave to fuggeft to the Court, that there is a variance in the fpelling of the name.

A *Certiorari* to remove a *feveral* indictment, would be bad, if a *joint* indictment were removed, a variation in the defcription of the party by a fingle letter has been held fatal.

Thefe are the objections which at prefent occur to me, I feel them to be of weight, and fuch as muft enforce the confideration of the Court, I fhould otherwife lament that I had exhaufted fo much of this, the laft day of Term, that it will be impoffible for the Court to hear the gentlemen who are on the fame fide with me, from whofe abilities and information the unfortunate gentleman at the bar would derive more advantage than from my poor exertions. I have only to offer my humble thanks to the Court for the patience with which they have heard my crude and undigefted thoughts upon a fubject of the laft importance, not only to the unfortunate gentleman at the bar, but to the adminiftration of the criminal juftice of the nation.

The *Court* afked if any other gentleman would point other objections.

Margin notes:
Rex
verfus
Keon.

12th Error

2 Hawk. 297

1ft Lord Raymond 609
2 Hawk. old ed 297-8, new ed. 423-4.

Mr.

Mr *Serjeant Hunt* faid he was prepared, and
proceeded to ftate, that the *Certiorari* was, as he
underftood it, directed to the Juftices of Affize
and the Coroner, and not returned by the perfons to whom directed, which he conceived was
error That the *Habeas Corpus* ought to have
borne Tefte on the day of the Return of the *Certiorari*, and the *Venire Facias* on the day of the
Return of the *Habeas Corpus* He then fuggefted,
that they were not tefted on thefe days, and of
courfe there was a *chafm* in the procefs, which
wrought a *difcontinuance* And that the *Venire*
being joint, the Court, with deference, were not
competent to fever the pannel, which had been
done—that the Prifoner was therefore mis-tried

Mr *Stanley*, in fupport of the different objec-
tions, cited 2 Salk 479. 2 Hawk 286-7.
Dogherty's Crown Circuit Affi Title *Certiorari*
Yelv 211-12 Cro Ja 254 Cro. Eliz 821 4
State Tri 640

Mr. *Bloffet* fuggefted that the indictment itfelf
was bad, the words " in the fear of God and
peace of our Lord the King," being omitted.

Mr. *Smith* alfo objected to the indictment, for
want of thefe words, " nor the duty of his allegiance confidering," which he held to be necef-
fiy, and the omiffion fatal

Mr. *O'Connor* infifted, that the word " before-
thought" being ufed inftead of " aforethought,"
vitiated the indictment Had the indictment been
in Latin, as formerly, *præcogitata* would have been
ufed, and *excogitata* has been held bad, and there
ought to be the fame precifion in the Englifh
Indictment

The

The Counfel for the Crown having declared themfelves not ready to anfwer the feveral objections *inftanter*, the Court remanded the prifoner, and directed him to be brought up the fecond day of next Term, 24th January, 1788.

24th JANUARY, 1788. *B R*

THE prifoner, Robert Keon, was brought up purfuant to the laft order, for the further argument of Counfel, on the motion in arreft of judgment

Deputy Clerk of the Crown.—Is Robert Keon here ?

Gaoler Yes

Serjeant *Hewitt* —I am of Counfel for the Prifoner, and in arguing the feveral points which I apprehend to be erroneous, I fhall omit every thing which does not appear to me to be of importance, and I fhall hope for the indulgence of the Court, not only becaufe it is a cafe of moment, as the life of a man is concerned in it, but becaufe it may regulate cafes of the kind hereafter

If the fame precifion be not adhered to here that is at the other fide of the water, it may perhaps be accounted for from this, that cafes of this kind feldom happen in this kingdom, and no Report of them is to be had, for in truth, except what may cafually be found in the

the notes of the Judges, not a trace of them remains They are consigned to oblivion

Previous to arguing the several errors, I shall first state what in my apprehension ought to be the order of the proceedings The *Record* should begin with a memorandum of the *Caption* of the indictment , which should be followed by the *indictment* itself , and then recite that the King for certain causes had directed the same to come before himself , next follows the process of *Capias*, then how the prisoner is brought up, next the *Arraignment*, his *Plea* and the *Issue* joined, then the *Venire Facias*, the day given, the Jury sworn, the *Verdict*, and then follows the *Judgment* , and these, as I take it, are the regular parts of a Record.

Having thus stated and submitted to the Court what ought to be the course of proceeding, I shall further submit what appears to me to be errors and defects on this Reccord   And

FIRST, the *Certiorari*, which issued at the request of the prosecutrix, bears Teste the last day of Easter Term, and is returnable in this Court after the Morrow of the Holy Trinity The *Habeas Corpus* is also directed to bring the bodies of Robert Keon and four others. However, before I shall observe on that, I shall premise, that if the *Certiorari* be mis-directed or mis-returned, the whole proceedings fall to the ground, nothing being removed The *Certiorari* is the foundation on which all the other proceedings are built · If this is erroneous, every thing subsequent to it is so likewise

Now I contend that the *Certiorari* is erroneous in these respects

1 It is mis-directed.

2. It

2. It is mif-returned

3. It is not returned on a proper Return day.

Rex
verfus
Keon.

If, fays *Hawkins*, a *Certiorari* be mif-directed nothing is removed

2 Hawk.
cap 27.
fect. 71.
new edit.
410.
old edit.
294.

This *Certiorari* is mif-directed—it is directed to the Clerk of the Crown, or Juftices of Peace, or any one who has the Record, and not to any one in particular —A *Certiorari* is in the nature of a *Mandamus*, and muft be directed to thofe, and thofe only who are to obey the Writ

Bradftreet, J —You have not feen the *Certiorari*. I will therefore read the direction of it for you, and it is, " To our Juftices of Affize and General Gaol Delivery held for the county of Lentrim, the Clerk of the Crown of the faid county, or his deputy there," and you will obferve that between the Juftices and the Clerk of the Crown, there is neither copulative or difjunctive.

Ante
pa. 12.

Serj *Hewitt* —If a mandamus be directed to the Mayor *and* Aldermen, it is wrong, and in the cafe to which I now allude, *Powell* fays, Writs ought to be directed to thofe, and thofe only, who are to execute them, or it would be immaterial —In that cafe there was fome degree of certainty, but here no certainty at all. If the Juftices are to return, the *Certiorari* ought to be directed to the Juftices alone If the Clerk of the Crown ought to return, it ought to be directed to him alone, and the cafe of the *King* againft the *Mayor* of *Abingdon* is in point

Salkeld
701

Salk.
Tit *Mandamus*

Bradftreet,

Rex versus Keon

Bradstreet, J —There are different Returns, when the Writ is directed to the Mayor and Recorder, when it is done by Deputy, it must be shewn by the Return that he has power to make a Deputy.

B 2 n ed
411 old
e t 290

B 4
Eiren. cap
7 p 515

Serj *Hewitt* —All the precedents I am able to find, says Hawkins, of *Certiorari*, are either directed to the Justices of the Peace for the county generally, or to some of them in particular by name, and not to the *Custos Rotulorum*, and according to *Lambard* they are never directed to him.

But supposing it were not *mis-directed*, I contend that it is improperly returned

There are two rules with regard to the Return of *Certiorari*

1st That every such Return must be under the seal of the inferior Court , and if the Court has no seal, then under any seal

2dly That it must be returned by the person to whom it was directed

Bradstreet, J —That was settled in the case of the *King* and *Percival* in this Court.

Serj *Hewitt*.—This Return is made, as I am instructed, by the Clerk of the Crown, and not by the Justices.

Bradstreet, J —That is the fact, and the mandatory part of the Writ is that you send under your seals or the seals of any of you

Serj *Hewitt* —This Return is by the Clerk of the Crown only, now this I contend is wrong ,
for

for it ought to be by both, and this you will find in the cafe of *Pie* againſt *Thrill* In that cafe it was directed to the *Cuſtos Rotulorum*, and not to the Juſtice, and held bad In the preſent cafe the Writ was directed to the Juſtices of the Peace, and returned by the Clerk of the Crown, and ſuppoſing him to keep the Records, on the authority of that cafe, and the cafe of *Elizabeth Aſt ley*, the Return is nought

Rex verſus Keon.
Hob 135.
2 Salk. 4⁻9

Bradſtreet, J—Have you any cafe to ſhew where the *Certiorari* is directed to the Juſtices of the Peace and the Clerk of the Crown, and the latter only returns it, that the Return is nought?

Serj *Hewitt* —If the *Certiorari* be not miſ-directed or miſ-returned, yet I contend that it is erroneous, becauſe it is not returnable on a common return-day

The *Certiorari* is an original writ, I admit that all original writs always iſſue out of Chancery. The original writ is the foundation upon which all ſubſequent proceſs is founded

The *Certiorari* removes the Record

The *Habeas Corpus* removes the Body

The writ of *Certiorari*, ſays Fitzherbert, is an original writ, and iſſueth ſometimes out of the Chancery, and ſometimes out of the King's Bench

Reg om. brev.

F N B 543 245.

Bennett, J.—Surely you do not mean to contend that a writ teſted by the Chief Juſtice is an original writ.

Serj. *Hewitt* —Whether it be an original or a judicial writ, I contend that it is not properly re-

M   turned

Rex
cer/is
Kcon

turned The Return is on Friday the 8th of June, which is not a day of general return, it ought to have been made returnable on the morrow of the Holy Trinity, or on the *quarto die post* In England, and I presume, the practice is the fame here, every *Certiorari* to remove an indictment shall be returned the first return-day of the term next after issued And this you will find settled in 1st of W and M.

1 Shov 336.

The next error, and which I rely on, affects the *Venire Facias*

It ought to be returnable on a common return day. The distinction in the books seems to be this, where the Jury-process is to a county where the Court of King's Bench sits then there is no need of fifteen days between the Teste and Return *Bumstead's Cafe* If the offence be committed in the county where the King's Bench sits, and the indictment be originally taken in the King's Bench, and the prisoner arraigned there, the Court may proceed *de die in diem*, but if the offence be committed in a foreign county, and indictment be removed from a foreign county, then there must be fifteen days between the Teste and Return of the *Venire Facias*, or other process

Cro El 448. 2 Str 825

2 Hale H. P.C. 260.

That the writ ought to be made returnable on a common return day, fee *Layer's Cafe*, and in that cafe the Chief Justice faid, that the Return being the octave of Saint Martin the trial must be on the *quarto die post* The *Venire Facias* was tested the 27th day of June, and ought to be returnable on the morrow of Saint Martin.

6 St. Tr.

Bennett, J—That would have been on Monday.

Serj.

Serj *Hewitt*—Then the trial would have been
on a Thursday. That the *Venire Facias* must be
returnable on a general return-day, is laid down
and settled in *Tutchin's* Case

Rex
versus
Keon
5 St Tr
349

The next objection is, that the *Venire Facias*
issued without any issue joined in this Court

Bennett, J—They had pleaded below before
the *Certiorari* issued.

Serj. *Hewitt*—I shall state what the proceedings
were. They were arraigned in the county of
Leitrim, and pleaded Not Guilty; a *Certiorari*
issued the last day of Easter term, the *Habeas
Corpus* issued twelve days after the issuing of the
joint *Venire*, which was tested on the day of the
return of the *Habeas Corpus* On the 16th day
of November they were brought up to the Court,
and had no notice whatsoever, previous to that
day, of the rule to take his trial, nor was the
prisoner present when the rule was made, and
on the authority of the *King* against *Baker*, he
ought to have been arraigned, and plead *de novo*.
The party is always admitted to plead *de novo*,
and to go to a trial upon an issue joined in this
Court Had the prisoner been arraigned here,
he might have waived the plea he had put in
below, he might have demurred here And
on the authority of this case, I apprehend that
the plea was waived by the *Certiorari*, which is
a *Supersedeas*.

Carth 6

Bradstreet, J.—To all subsequent proceedings.

Serj

Rex
verſus
Keon

2 H H
P. C 224

Serj *Hewitt* —He had a right to claim the liberty of pleading *de novo*, ſimilar to the caſe in Hale

Suppoſing him arraigned, and that he had waived his plea, no iſſue could have been joined and if there were no iſſue joined, what then becomes of the *Venire Facias* ?—The *Venire Facias* is to try an iſſue joined

I ſhall cite ſome caſes which have been furniſhed as to this point, by Mr *Adair*, the Recorder of London, and, as I am inſtructed, one of them was before Mr. Juſtice *Gould*.

The *King* againſt Doctor *Shipley*, Dean of St *Aſaph* He was arraigned at Wrexham, and the Indictment being removed by *Certiorari*, he pleaded *de novo* in the Court of King's Bench

In the Caſe of the *King* and *Aylett*, he was indicted for perjury, the Indictment was removed, and he pleaded *de novo*

In the Caſe of the *King* and *Ward*, who was tried in Eſſex in the year 1786, before Mr Juſtice *Gould*, he was indicted for felony, and the Indictment was removed, and he pleaded *de novo*

Bradſtreet, J——Shew me a Caſe where a man convicted below made this objection

Bennett, J——In ſuch a Caſe, might there not be two iſſues joined, one of Law and one of Fact

Serj *Hewitt* ——There is another objection, which is, that the Rule for his trial was made in his abſence, and on the authority of the *King* and *Johnſon*, no Rule ought to be made in the abſence of the Priſoner.

* Str. 825

The

The laſt objection, and with which I ſhall conclude, is, the ſevering the trial, and putting Robert Keon on his trial without the reſt of the priſoners, though there was a joint *Venire* againſt all, and Hale ſays, " It ſeems that in Caſe of an Indictment, though it be the King's ſuit, if once a *Venire Facias* iſſues joint, there cannot iſſue ſeveral *Venire Facias*, nor a ſeveral *Tales*, which in many caſes may much delay, nay fruſtrate the trial " The diſtinction is, that before Juſtices of gaol delivery the trials may be ſevered, but in no others, and the Juſtices did not ſit as a Court of gaol delivery, for I admit, if the Court of King's Bench went into another county, they might then, by their mere precept, award the Jury and ſever the pannel, but not otherwiſe

Mr *Recorder* —This is an application to arreſt judgment for erroneous proceedings and a miſtrial, and many queſtions of law are involved in this motion —Before a man is liable to have judgment pronounced againſt him for a debt due to the party, or to the public, he muſt be regularly impleaded and proceeded againſt, and what are regular and ſufficient pleadings and proceedings, is matter of law.

This indictment was found in a foreign country, and for its removal hither a *Certiorari* iſſued laſt Eaſter Term, but that *Certiorari* was *not* made returnable on the morrow of the Holy Trinity The Prime Serjeant and Serjeant Hewitt, have argued that that *Certiorari* was miſ-directed and miſ-returned, and if they have eſtabliſhed either allegation, it follows, that nothing has been removed by that *Certiorari*, and that all the proceedings here are void

It

Rex versus Keon.

2 H H P C 264

1 Shower 336

2 Hawk. c 27, ſect 77

Rex
versus
Keon.

It now appears that the *Certiorari* was directed
" To the Justices of Assize, Clerk of the Crown,
or his deputy ,' and although there is not a copulative between the Justices of Assize and Clerk
of the Crown, yet as that addition would make
its direction right and legal, the Court will understand that such is the direction, and then the
Return made by the Clerk of the Crown alone, is
insufficient, and it is not averred that he alone
had the custody of the *Record*, and although the
Certiorari and its *Return* do not compose a part
of the indictment roll, yet the Court will look
into this part of the proceedings and see whether
the errors assigned do exist.

Layer's
Cas., 6
St. Trial.

The *Venire* was awarded in Trinity Term last,
returnable on a day certain, to wit, the 16th of
November

Bacon
Abr Tit.
Juries,
236.

This *Venire* must have been awarded on the roll,
otherwise it is unfounded, and if such award on
the roll was never made, I humbly contend it was
a mis-award, and that for more than one reason.

At or before the time of that award made, the
prisoner was not in the Court, or so much as in
the county where the Court sat

At or before the time of that award made, the
prisoner had not pleaded in this Court, and no
issue was here joined, and the prisoner had never
had an opportunity of pleading here given him.
Awarding the *Venire* and fixing its return on a day
certain, was appointing a day for the trial, and
issuing a *Venire*, and appointing a day for trial
before a prisoner is brought up, and whilst he is
in a foreign county, and before he has pleaded
such plea as he must abide by is pregnant with so
much legal inconvenience that it cannot be regular—it must be erroneous Until a record of a
foreign county is brought in, the Court will not
make any order concerning it, but to bring it in ,

until

until a prisoner in a foreign county is brought up, the Court will not make any other order to affect him save for the bringing him up, until the Court has a direct and immediate dominion over both the man and the indictment, jury process cannot regularly go forth or a day for trial be appointed, otherwise a foreign county may be nearly depopulated of its freeholders, sent hither to try a man become insane—who has escaped—who has died—who has been pardoned—or who may, of common right, plead in abatement or demur to the indictment. In any of which, and in many similar cases that may be supposed, the services of a Jury would not be wanting.

The *Venue* was mis-awarded, as there was not then any plea pleaded, or issue joined, in this Court, between the King and the prisoner, and if the *Record* was regularly made up below and returned, no plea or issue joined could appear upon it.

Bradstreet, J.—There is a plea returned, and issue joined by the Clerk of the Crown on the *Record*, returned to us by the Coroner.

Mr. *Recorder*.—Then such plea or joinder of issue ought not to have been entered on the *Record* or returned, the pleading of prisoner at the assizes was *ore tenus* and *instanter*, and although such mode of pleading be right and regular when an immediate trial is to follow, yet the law does not require that such plea or joinder of issue should be entered on the *Record* at the assizes, or returned on the *Record* when there has not been a trial or indictment below, it was irregular to return on the *Record* a plea and issue by which the prisoner was not concluded, and which he might waive

4 Burr 2005

4 Viner T. t Corn. fo 362 the King v Carpenter.

Carthew 6

Rex
verfus
Keon

waive of common right, and at his pleafure, fince no trial or indictment was had below, arraignment here was necefiary, as well to give the Court judicial knowledge of the man named in the indictment, as to give the prifoner notice of the charge he was to defend himfelf againft. Now, what legal intimation had the Prifoner of his trial for his life here, until the Clerk of the Crown put him to his challenges on the 16th of November—The law does not require that he fhould have any notice of the *Certiorari*, nor can the Court prefume he had any notice of it.

The law does not require that he fhould have any notice of the iffuing of the *Habeas Corpus*, nor is the Sheriff who acts under it bound to produce it to the Prifoner, or affign to the Prifoner the caufe, or the purpofe for which he is removed; and fo the Court will not prefume that the Prifoner in this Capital can have any notice of the purpofe for which he was here tranfmitted.

And as to the *Venire* awarded, executed, and returned in the abfence, and without the privity of the Prifoner, he cannot be prefumed to have had any the leaft notice of that, and fince from none of thefe proceedings could the Prifoner have had a legal intimation of his trial before the 16th of November, what other fufficient notice, or notice which the law in a capital cafe confiders to be fufficient, has he had?

Bennett, J.—Suppofe he had put off his trial at one Affizes to the next, what knowledge would the next Judges have of the Prifoner, and muft he again be arraigned to give him notice he was to be put on his trial?

Mr *Recorder*—If his trial was fo to be poftponed, it muft be fo put off in his prefence and hearing,

ing, and that is notice of trial to him direct; and
although the Judge who prefides at next Affizes
may be a different man, yet the Court is the fame,
and fo has judicial knowledge of him, there is nothing then left to doubt and uncertainty. But
againft a Prifoner removed from a foreign county,
there may be more indictments than one, both
here and there, and for various offences, and fo
after his removal, and in a convenient time before his trial, he fhould have had legal notice of
the accufation he was to defend, as no man fhould
be put to anfwer for all the criminal acts of his
life at a moment's warning

The Court is particularly careful in giving a
Prifoner, confined even under civil procefs, notice of the Declaration, and its contents, before
rules to plead fhall be entered up againft him,
and notice of trial, but when the life of a man
is to be decided on, the Court will give him notice of trial with its own voice.

The *Venire* was, I fubmit to your Lordfhips,
for thefe reafons, mif-awarded, but although it
was not fo, yet in this cafe it fhould have been
made returnable on a general *return day*, and
not on a day *certain*

Bradftreet, J —Have you fearched for precedents of the practice here.

Mr. *Recorder* —My Lord, we have not —I do
not confider it a matter of practice, but a matter of
law, and if the practice here has not been con-
formable to law, it fhould be corrected —That
this *Venire* fhould have been fo returnable, the authorities are all one way, and not even a *dictum* of
any Judge againft it.—So in the *King* and *Roberts*,
fo in *Tuchin's* cafe, fo in *Knightly's* cafe.—And
the

Rex verfus Keon.

2 Sh. 285.

1 Wilfon 77

5 St. Tr. 766

4 St Tr 547

N

Rex
versus
Keon.

the Judges there, speaking of a *Venue* otherwise
returnable, do not merely say it would be irregular but erroneous —Besides, the Jury at that time
arrayed under this *Venue* were excepted to, and
challenged by the Prisoner, and that challenge is
now on the *Record* before the Court.

Bradstreet, J —If these exceptions have not
been made your cause of challenge, you cannot avail yourself of them.

Mr *Recorder* —I admit the challenge was not
for this special cause, but this I submit, is matter of substance erroneous on the face of the writ,
for which we have a right to have judgment,
to quash an array made under that writ.

The last matter which I shall humbly contend to be erroneous in this *Record*, is, that
this is an Indictment from a foreign county ; the
Jury process by writ , the writ a joint one, to
return a Jury to try five persons, and yet, the
pannel was severed, and a several trial had of
one prisoner, without the prisoner's consenting
to the severance

The Court will carefully distinguish this case
from that of an Indictment of the county, where
the Court sits—the distinction is obvious —No
doubt, this is the Supreme Court of criminal
jurisdiction, and is a Court of general gaol delivery for every county in Ireland, but by this
I do not mean to say, that whilst this Court sits
here, there is a Court of general gaol delivery
sitting for every county in Ireland, at that time ;
or that this Court is now a Court of general
gaol delivery for each county in Ireland, for
all purposes—If that be so no Court of general

ral gaol delivery could fit in any county in Ireland in term time, but I apprehend that although this Court muft clofe and filence all other Courts of general gaol delivery into which it may enter, yet that even now a Court of general gaol delivery might be legally fitting in the county of Leitrim. In the county where this Court fits for the time being, its procefs through the fame county cannot be lefs effectual for expediting juftice, than the procefs of other Courts of general gaol delivery. But when it fits for the trial of an offence and indictment of a foreign county, another practice is to take place—there muft be fifteen days between the Tefte and Return of each procefs, in fuch cafes the Jury Procefs is not by a general precept, or particular precept, but is *by Writ*. When the Jury Procefs is awarded to the Sheriff of the county where the Court of general gaol delivery fits, his pannel arrayed under the award of the Court is joint, or feveral, as the ends of juftice may require. All is in the power of the Juftices, and they may, in making up the Record, model the award on the Roll fo as to prevent error, becaufe in fuch cafe they are not fettered by the ftrict formality of a Writ. But, I humbly contend, that when this Court can only communicate with the Sheriff of a foreign county by Writ, that the King or the profecutor muft elect, before the *Venire* iffues, whether that *Venire* fhall be joint and feveral, and that if a joint *Venire* fhall iffue, it fhall not be joint and feveral at the election of the profecutor afterwards. If fuch *Venires* are to be confidered joint and feveral, how can we reconcile to fenfe or reafon the doctrine of Hale and Hawkins, that after a joint *Venire* there cannot be a feveral *Diftringas* or *Tales*, or why

were

Rex
verfus
Keon.

2 Inf.
560

2 Hale,
Pl C
2

Edw.
to 27,
28

Tale,
434

Rex
verfus
Keon.

Kelyng 9

were several *Venires*, or several pannels, returned, if a pannel coming from a foreign county,
by virtue of a joint *Venire*, can be severed?
Now, by the severance of this pannel, returned
under a joint *Venire*, there has been a discontinuance.

Lord Chief Juftice.—How do you make that
appear?

Mr. *Recorder*—My Lord, I humbly contend it
appears thus.—A *Venire* was awarded between
the King and five persons jointly, and a joint *Venire* issued accordingly; and the Sheriff has arrayed and returned his pannel between the King and
five prisoners jointly, and then the Court has ordered the same Jurors to be arrayed between the
King and *Robert Keon* alone, and the Jury is
discharged as to the rest. A several pannel returned by the Sheriff to a joint *Venire*, would be
no Return to it, and a Jury so returned could
not try any thing; and to legalize such a Return
the Court muft make a different award of a several Writ, but that you could not do *inftanter*,
or without fifteen days between the Tefte and
Return of the Writ, and as the proceeding was
by Writ, you cannot mold and model that Writ
and its Return on the moment, so as to accommodate it to the occasion.

Bradftreet, J——Have you any authority to
shew that Juftices of gaol delivery cannot issue a
Writ into their own county, if they are content
to be so long delayed.

Mr *Recorder*—Though they should issue such
Writ, yet after its Return, if the ends of juftice
so required, they might quash it, and on an immediate

mediate award adopt the same Return, and so no error or discontinuance would appear, but in the case before the Court at present, if the Court has in effect quashed a joint *Venire*, and awarded a several one, and made the Sheriff of Leitrim, for the first time, array in Dublin a several pannel between the *King* and *Robert Keon* alone, all this I submit was not a work to be legally done in a moment, where the Jury Process was by Writ, and the Indictment of a foreign county.

For these reasons, I humbly contend the Judgment should be arrested.

Rex
versus
Keon

[Here the Court having settled to hear another Counsel for the Prisoner, in reply to what might be said on behalf of the Crown, the Counsel for the prosecution were called on to answer the objections.]

Mr *Duquery*, as Counsel for the Crown, said, the Counsel for the Prisoner have objected to the *Direction* and the *Return* of the *Certiorari*.

The direction is to " our Justices of Assize, the Clerk of the Crown, or his Deputy."

That I conceive to be the proper direction of a *Certiorari*. It may be directed to the Justices, or to the Officer having, by virtue of his office, the custody of the Record so is the uniform course of precedents, and in 2 *Hawk* 411 it is said, that the usual course of precedents is the best guide whereby to judge of the matter If well directed, it is well returned, for the return exactly follows the direction. The Officer who had the custody of the Record, has returned it as the writ called upon him to to do. These objections appear to have but little weight. Others are made which deserve more serious consideration.

It

It is objected, that the *Certiorari* should have been made returnable on a general return day No authority has been cited on the other side in support of this assertion, and I have not been able to find any The precedents in *Fitzherbert* are against the position The Writs are there made returnable " *sine dilatione*," and upon good reason, because the *Certiorari* stops all the proceedings of the Court below , it would therefore tend to the delay of justice, to bind the return of Writs of *Certiorari* to the general return day. When the superior Court stops by this Writ the inferior Court from dispensing justice, it should have a power to proceed itself forthwith, which could not be if the Writ of *Certiorari* was returnable on a general return day. The Writ of *Certiorari* in this case is not an *original Writ*, if issued out of *this Court*, and not out of *Chancery*. There are different modes of removing the Records The Court of Chancery may issue its Writ of *Certiorari* returnable into its *own Court*, and then by Mittimus transmit the tenor of the Record here or the Court of Chancery may issue the *Certiorari*, and make it returnable at will into this Court , or lastly, this Court may issue its own Writ of *Certiorari*, as is the case here , and the *Certiorari* which issues out of this Court is not an *original* Writ, as the Writ out of Chancery is This distinction will explain why Writs of *Certiorari*, issuing out of Chancery, are returnable on a general return day, and other Writs of *Certiorari* on a day certain And the doctrine on the Return laid down by the other side, if it applies at all to Writs of *Certiorari*, applies only to the Writ which issues out of Chancery, and not the Writ of the King's Bench And this distinction is clearly taken by Lord *Hale*.

H P. C.
415

But

But it has been objected, that the Writ of *Venire* in this case should have been returnable on a general return day

What Writs must be returnable on a general *return day*, and what may be made returnable on a *day certain*, I do not find any where fully ascertained

The origin of days in *Bank* is certainly very antient , as far as I can collect, it arose when the Court of *Chancery* became, on the division of the jurisdiction of the *Aula Regia*, the *Officina Brevium* for the other Courts The Clerks in Chancery then had the Return of the Writs , and at first made them returnable at such days as they or the Justices thought fit, this was a public inconvenience, and embarrassed the administration of justice To remedy this, Days in Bank, upon which days alone *original Writs* should be returnable, seem to have taken their rise.

If this be the true origin of days in Bank, (and *Reeves* in his History of the English Law justifies this presumption, then the rules relative to Writs returnable on days in bank, do not apply to Writs issuing out of this Court, as the *Venire* did in this case In all the statutes which regulate the Return of Writs, *Hen* III. to *Geo* I the power of the Court to make Writs returnable on *days certain* is *recognized* and *preserved*, indeed what writs may be returned on days certain are not in those statutes specified

It does not appear that the rules relative to general return days, or days in bank, are applicable to Writs issuing of this Court in *criminal cases* The *criminal jurisdiction* of the Court of King's Bench was never intended to be narrowed by these days in bank The inconvenience might

might be serious to confine the Return of the *Venire*, even as to foreign counties, in criminal cases, and consequently trials in such cases, to three or four stated days in each term

This Court was originally intended to administer justice in *criminal cases*; and such a rule as is contended for, would considerably abridge that jurisdiction

If these days in bank are the proper days of return for *original* Writs, or for Writs in *civil* cases, the rules which govern the Return of such Writs do not apply to the Return of the *Venire* here, which is a *judicial* Writ in a *criminal* case

6 St. T. In *Layer's* case the point determined was, that the appearance of the Jury was good on the *quarto die post* I take that to be the ancient rule *of practice* in England, and so the Court there seemed to consider it *Here* the usage of the Court is otherwise, it is to try *on the Return day*, and to make the Return on a *day certain* and the *usage of the Court* in such matters makes the *law of the Court* The dernier resort is now in the lords of this kingdom, and we must be governed by our own *antient usage*

Even if the King's Bench of *England* was to determine this on a Writ of Error, that Court would require to be certified as to the usage here, and upon that certificate would determine that the Return of the *Venire* was right.

It has been objected that the prisoner should have been brought into this Court to plead again before he was put upon his trial, upon what principle I cannot see He had pleaded " Not " Guilty" in the Court below, that is the most beneficial plea for the prisoner, he had put himself upon the country on that issue, and the Crown had joined in the issue with the prisoner.

In

In this ftage the Record was removed; by the removal the proceedings are brought here, and ftand in the fame plight and condition as they were in the inferior Court below, the *Certiorari* does not unravel any of the proceedings had below, but commands them to be certified here as far as they have gone. It might as well be argued that *after conviction* he fhould be arraigned *de novo*, no rule of law, or indeed of reafon fays that a prifoner, who has pleaded " Not " Guilty" in the inferior Court, muft be brought to plead again at the bar of this Court. If he pleaded again, and the former plea was contradictory to the latter, two inconfiftent pleas would appear on the Record, which would be Error. But having pleaded " Not Guilty," and puting himfelf on his country, the Court had nothing remaining to do, but to award the *Venire* to call in the Jury, upon whom the Prifoner had put himfelf for his trial. The Prifoner here has not been deprived of any privilege which he could exercife. As foon as the Jury was returned, he then was brought up to the bar of the Court, to challenge the Array or the Polls, as he thought expedient, that was the *firft right* he could exercife after he pleaded, and that right he did exert in its fulleft extent.

It is ftated to be error that the *Venire* was *joint,* and the pannel *fevered*. Here too I muft obferve that no authority has been quoted to prove that the Court of King's Bench cannot, where the *Venire* is joint, fever the pannel. Principle is certainly againft the pofition ——— It is admitted on all hands, that Juftices of gaol delivery can fever the pannel, and in Lord *Sanchar's* Cafe, it is faid, that this Court has all the powers of gaol delivery. As foon as the proceedings are removed here by *Certiorari*, I conceive that you have

Recordis Recor.

9 Co.

Rex versus Keon

have every power and legal discretion in the trial of offences so removed from a foreign county, that you have as to indictments found in the county where you sit.

It would be strange doctrine to establish, that Justices of Gaol Delivery, or of Oyer and Terminer, have a discretion vested in them, after a joint Inquest awarded against many Prisoners, to sever the pannel, and yet that this Court has no such power, requires some clear authority to support a position so strongly militating against general principles. If after a joint Inquest was awarded against five persons indicted for the same offence, it was against any sound principle of law, or any rule of justice, to sever the pannel, the Justices of Gaol Delivery should not have such a power invested in them, any more than another Court of criminal jurisdiction. If it was illegal or unfair for the Prisoner to sever a joint Inquest, it would be equally illegal and improper, whatever may be the constitution, of the Court in which he stands his trial, the only difference is, that the error would appear on the Record in this case, and not when done by Justices of Gaol Delivery.

One principal reason why, though the Inquest be joint, the pannel may be severed, is, because, though Indictments may be joint, *Offences* are in their nature *several*. Each man's crime is in itself a separate crime, and every Indictment, though joint in its form, is in law a several Indictment for each, and the Inquest impannelled on such Indictment, may be considered as a *several Inquest* for each Prisoner.

Bradstreet, J.—All offences are joint and several, except *conspiracy*, which can be only *joint*,

and

and *perjury*, which can only be a *several* offence

Mr *Duquery*—Another reason why a pannel may be severed is, because prisoners, though jointly indicted, and the *venue* be joint, may *sever in their Challenges*, and the man challenged by one, shall be *drawn against all*, it was therefore necessary to invest the Court with a power to sever the pannel, or there might often occur an entire failure of justice. This is well explained in *Salisbury's* Case

Fairfort, C. J.—He complains that he might have had the benefit of an hundred challenges by means of the joint *venue* against the five, and he says this was a hardship

Mr *Duquery*—The law as now settled intends not to allow the Prisoner more than twenty peremptory challenges—And that affords an argument why the Court should have a power to sever the pannel. If the consequence of denying the Court the power of severing the pannel, would be to give an advantage to the prisoners of eighty or one hundred challenges, this is a further reason why the Court should have such a power; because otherwise persons jointly indicted, by severing in their challenges, would have much larger privileges in that respect than one prisoner taking his separate trial, which the law cannot intend

But is that an advantage? I conceive, with deference, no. The Prisoner may wish that a Juror may pass upon his life, to whom the rest object. So far, therefore, from being a benefit, it may be an injury. Twenty peremptory chal-

lenges

Rex
v.
Keon

lenges are the right of each Prisoner, and no more, to enlarge that privilege, would be to deviate from the rule of Law

I submit, upon these grounds, the motion in arrest of judgment not to be well founded

Court.—Remand the Prisoner, and let him be brought up to-morrow

---

Friday, January 25, 1788 *B R*

Robert Keon was brought up, pursuant to the order of yesterday

Mr *Caldbeck*, of Counsel for the Crown—A great many objections have been made on behalf of the Prisoner, and a great many have been given up They are now reduced to the objections made to the *Certiorari*, and the *Venire*—the mode of his trial, (he being tried alone, in the absence of four others)—that the time of his trial had been appointed in his absence, and that he ought to have pleaded *de novo*

I cannot agree that either the law or the practice of this country is the same as in England, and there are many instances where our law and our practice are more advantageous, and better suited to the furtherance of justice It is necessary here to distinguish between the law of the land and the practice of the Court

The great object of the law is the punishment of offences to deter others, by example, from the like transgressions, and the object of practice and process is, that innocence and the merits of the

the Prisoner may be fairly and regularly brought before the Court

The present presumption is, that Mr Keon is guilty—He was found so after a long and impartial trial of his country. The justice of the Court, the safety of the Country, demand that guilt shall not escape, were it otherwise, it would be *miseri ordo puniens*.

In capital case courts often have allowed objections of a very trifling kind, and it is now attempted to lay that down as a general rule, but gentlemen would do well to recollect, that such objections have been permitted, not only as it is urged in *favorem vitæ*, that a criminal should escape, but in *ordsi f atiorem justitia*, that the merit might be tried, being favoured only to avoid conviction upon outlawry, and afterwards misapplied to cases in arrest of judgment.

There was an ineffectual attempt to try the Prisoner in the county of Leitrim. On the indictment there he pleaded Not Guilty in the usual manner, and this plea is called, by the other side, *short-hand*. Nicknames avail nothing. The Clerk of the Crown's notes are intelligible by every man of law, and it is ineffectual to cavil at the Record, it not being as yet made up; and when it is, perhaps they will find every thing on it that ought to be contained in it.

When the *Certiorari* issued, it was directed " to the Justices of Assize, the Clerk of the " Crown, or his Deputy," and the command is to transmit the Indictment, and all things touching it. Gentlemen were right in saying, that it must be returned by the person to whom it is directed. Is it necessary to do more than to read the Writ? It is *quasi* two separate *Certioraris*: for it is directed to the Justices, and to the Clerk of the Crown, without any copulative, and the

Record,

Record, for any thing that appears, must have been in the custody of other men —— It is transmitted by the Clerk of the Crown, who had the custody of it. If the Certiorari was improperly directed, if it were improperly returned, it would be as if not returned at all.

It is said that there is no plea. Does this require any answer, but to read the Record. It is said there is no *similiter*. Whatever the practice may be in misdemeanors, it is not necessary for the Clerk of the Crown to join in the *similiter* in capital cases.

Bradstreet, J.—You need not labour that, for the Clerk of the Crown appears to have joined in it on the *Record*.

Mr *Caldbeck*—It is said that the *Certiorari* ought to be returned on a common return day. This *Blackstone* attributes to the sturdy spirit of our ancestors, who disdained to obey the mandates of our courts of justice to the letter, or to attend in less than four days after the time appointed. Can the same reason apply to an officer of the Crown, or can he be supposed to possess the refractory spirit of the ancient *Britons*?

The Court considers not, when it fixes trials at bar, whether they are to be had on a day *certain*, or on a *common return-day*, and the practice of the Court is the law of the Court, and after long usage the Court will not shake it —— The practice of this Court must be guided by itself, and not by that of *Westminster-Hall*. If the practice be as the gentlemen on the other side have alledged, where are the precedents from off your file. I lament as much as the learned

Serjeant

Servant that there are not attentive reporters of cases here as well as in *Great Britain* Has any search been made by the gentlemen on the other side, to shew that the practice here was as they say? If I am not misinstructed, there are no such precedents, but it is their duty to shew that there are Great diligence, I am told, has been used in this and in another kingdom, and what has been the effect of it—They could not find the practice they contend for in either

As to pleading again, I confess it appears to me to be something like what, in another kingdom, would be called a *blunder*, and if practised here, a *bull* I believe the Prisoner could not be permitted to withdraw his plea, without the leave of the Attorney-General, and is it likely where the general issue has been pleaded, that he would consent? Suppose he should be called upon to plead again, and then stood mute, your Lordship then must pass sentence of death upon him, as standing *mute* of *malice*, though you knew he had before pleaded *Not Guilty*, and that his plea had been returned to you upon record For is it permissible to presume, that the Court of the Crown should mutilate the *Record?*

This *Certiorari* was to remove a separate indictment, and it removed a joint one.

Bennett, J.—That objection was given up

Mr *Caldbeck*—They object to the *Venire*, and assert there was no award of it upon the roll The answer to this is, there is no roll as yet made up —It is asserted, that it issued before the *Habeas Corpus* was returned or returnable, and before the prisoner was in Court, and that he never was in Court before the day of his trial

Bradstreet

Rex
versus
Keon.

Bradstree, J—The fact is, the *Return* of the *Habeas Corpus* is the last day of term, and the Prisoner was brought up some time in vacation.

Mr *Caldwell*—All that is necessary is that in construction of law, he should be in custody.

It is objected that there was a joint *Venire* to try five persons, and only one was tried.

It cannot be said that there was not a Jury to try Mr Robert Keon. It cannot be so with regard to him—His trial proceeded on the appointed day at the return of the writ—It is alledged that his being tried alone amounts to a discontinuance, what it may amount to should the other four be tried, will be the question of another day.

It is admitted that the power of severing the pannel is in the Justices of Gaol Delivery, but not in the Court of King's Bench—Was there not a time when there was no Commission of Gaol Delivery——Were not these Commissioners framed in ease of the Court of King's Bench. Is not their power derived, does it not spring from this Court, the great Court of Gaol Delivery of the nation? and shall the branch have more strength then the tree that bears it, the sucker more power than the root from which it springs?—Would it be for the advancement of justice, should the Sheriff return but twenty four jurors on the *Venire*, as was contended on the other side? Suppose one or two offenders put off their trial on a substantial affidavit, shall not the rest be tried?—No, not 'till the next Term——The next Term the rule is still the same, all must be tried or none: one is sick and unable to attend, *Essoign* would thus beget *Essoign*,
and

Essoign, and no trial could ever be had   If then
the rule contended for contains this grofs abfur-
dity, and if Commiffioners of Gaol Delivery
could fever the trials, but the Court of King's
Bench cannot, it would be more for the convenience of government, and more for the furtherance of juftice, to have the trial in the inferi-
or than in the fuperior Court.

It is faid he was not in Court when his trial was
appointed, and that in a capital cafe no rule can
be made but in the prefence of the Prifoner —
This rule is much too large as it has been laid
down   If not how was the *Certiorari* moved for
when he was in Leitrim Gaol?——How could
the firft rule be made to bring him up to this
Court, when he had been committed on the
Habeas Corpus? It has been even held, but they
are authorities I am afhamed to cite, but they
may be found in the State Trials, that it is not
neceffary that a prifoner fhould even have notice
of the day on which he is to be tried

Where any queftion of law may arife it muft
be put in the prefence of the prifoner, that he
may *object* if it be not truly put   In the appointing the trial was it neceffary for him to be
in Court? Could he make any legal objection to
it? —Certainly not

The true reafon why he is prefent on thefe
occafions is, that the Court may be fure of him,
and in cafe his guilt appears, may fend him into
cuftody.

Suppofing he had this right of pleading again
——Did he claim it, did he ever afk to withdraw his original plea until after he was tried?
——He was certainly in Court when he was
tried, nor was it for want of enough being faid
on his behalf, that he did not demand it as a

P   right

2 St. Tr.
720, Lord
Cornwal-
ls's cafe
5 st Tr
760 Lord
Warwick's
Corolls's
trial
St Tr 4
to. 145,
377. 544,
——— 968
——1227.
2 Burro.
930.
3 Burro.
1-56

right to plead again—But is it now for him to say that he might have pleaded? Perhaps if there be these errors which are fuggefted, if they had been taken notice of fo early as the Statutes *Jeofails* do not extend to criminal cafes, the Court would have ordered the profecutor to commence *de novo*

Are thefe objections made to any thing which prevents a trial of the merits?—If they are, in the name of God, let the proceedings all be fet afide.——But if they are made for a contrary purpofe, your Lordfhip will look into them with eagles eyes for a very different end. Does the innocence or guilt of the Prifoner depend on the direction of the *Certiorari*, or on the *Return*, whether it is by the Juftices of Affize, or Clerk of the Crown? Would he be innocent if the *Venue* had been returnable on a common *Return*? and muft a Jury find him guilty right or wrong, if they be fummoned to try him on a certain day? or would the Jury upon the fame evidence have acquitted him if he had been tried in company with the other four, who are indicted for the fame offence?

Let us now confider what advantage would accrue to the Prifoner fhould he now prevail — Would it clear him of the crime of which he ftands convicted? would it fet him free from all danger of punifhment?——No, it would be but to bring the County of Leitrim again into the Hall of the King's Bench—again to examine the fame witneffes—again to have a like verdict found and recorded

But this would take up time and *de morte hominis nulla eft cunctatio longa*

So fhould it be indeed of innocent unoffending men, but with what propriety, with what
decency

decency can this rule be applied to him, who gave his unoffending, his offended fellow creature no longer time than served for the pulling of a trigger. Justice indeed is truly said to be lame, but I hope the Prisoner in this will find he hopes in vain to tire her by delay.

If then form, unessential form, ought not to prevail over the weeping justice of the nation—if objections are not to be favoured, that I am bold to say were never made at the Bar of this Court before—if the life, the impunity of a convicted criminal, is not to be preferred to the safety of mankind, to be preferred to that example which the law demands aloud, and all good men must acquiesce in, while they lament the occasion and the necessity that calls for it in this case, then must not the judgment on this verdict be arrested, and one man must fall a victim to his own violence in future, that all others may hope in future to breathe in peace.

Mr *Smith*, Counsel for the Prisoner.—I lament most sincerely that the duty of replying in this case was not taken up by some other of the gentlemen concerned on the same side with me, to whom it more peculiarly belonged, and who might have discharged it with more advantage to the Prisoner at the bar.

The first objection I shall make is, that the *Certiorari* in this case has been *mis-returned.* I admit it to have been legally directed. The direction, as I understood it from the Court, is, " to the Justices of Assize, the Clerk of the Crown, or his Deputy." The disjunctive seems only to apply as between the Clerk of the Crown and his Deputy, and therefore I conceive that the Justices of Assize, or one of them, ought to

P 2   have

Rex
versus
Keon

have joined in the Return with the Clerk of the Crown, or his Deputy. And the words of the Writ, viz. " and this Writ you cause to be returned under your seal, or the seal of any of you," shew clearly that the word *you* must be considered as plural, as if it were translated *Præcipimus vobis ut sub sigillo vestro vel sigillo alicujus vestrum, &c.*

Bennet, J.—The words of the Writ are, " we therefore command you and every of you."

Mr. ——.—This, I contend, strengthens the position, that the construction ought to be plural, and from thence I infer, that though the Writ might be returned under the seal of any one of the persons to whom it was directed, yet the preceptive part of the Writ made it necessary that the Justices of Assize, or one of them, should join in making the Return.

My next objection is, that the *Certiorari* is not made returnable on a common day, but on a day certain. " The *Certiorari* is an original writ, and sometimes issues out of Chancery and sometimes out of the Court of King's Bench," says Fitzherbert. If it were to be considered as, in strictness, an original writ, ought certainly to have been made returnable on a common day, and ought to have fifteen days between its Teste and Re-

9 Co Rep turn, *Sander's Case.*——But I do not myself consider the Writ of *Certiorari*, when it issues from the King's Bench, as an original writ, it certainly is not—it is judicial; but it must not have fifteen days between its Teste and Return, and seems to partake of the essence, and to pos-

6 St Tr sess the *material* attributes of an *original* writ. *Lye's Case.*

The

Rex
versus
Keon
F N. B.
554

The *Venire* subsequent to it must be made returnable on a *common* return day, which seems to warrant the inference, that the *Certiorari* itself ought also to be made returnable on a *common* day.

But it may be said, that the day on which a writ is made returnable is a matter of practice, and not of law. I deny it. I say, it is of the *essence* of the writ, and is a pure question of law. Suppose the *Certiorari* here had issued out of Chancery, and had therefore been a strict original writ, could the Court hesitate to say, that making it returnable on a day *certain* would have been clearly error in point of law.

My next objection is, that the Prisoner was not, before the jury-process issued, *actually* brought up and arraigned at the bar of this Court, so as to have been admitted, if he chose, to waive his plea below, and plead *de novo* here. And so is the law laid down in the case of the *King* against *Baker*, which seems also Carth. 6. to accord with reason and justice, for though the Prisoner, by pleading as he did below, submitted to the jurisdiction of that Court, yet he never submitted to the jurisdiction of this Court, and ought not to be precluded from pleading to its jurisdiction.

Suppose the *Certiorari* had been clearly mis-directed or mis-returned, would not he have a right to plead such mis-direction or mis-return, and then of course nothing was removed —If I am told that the Court would not permit him to plead to the jurisdiction as being a dilatory plea, I answer that the argument is not thereby relaxed, (supposing the position true) for the Court cannot know what new plea he may plead, unless he has been arraigned, and put to plead *de novo*.

In

Rex qverfus Keon.

In the cafe of the Dean of *Saint Afaph*, removed from Wrexham, by *Certiorari*, the Dean was admitted to plead again

In the *King* and *Aylett*, the indictment was for perjury, and removed, and *Aylett* pleaded again

In the *King* and *Ward*, at Eflex, before Mr. *Juftice Gould*, the Record was removed by *Certiorari*, and the Prifoner was permitted to plead *de novo*

But here the Jury Procefs iffued before the Prifoner ever was *actually* in Court—nor was he ever *actually* in Court until the day of his trial—So that not only the Rule laid down in *Caribew*, of always admitting the Prifoner to plead *de novo*, but alfo the Rule laid down in the *King* against *Johnfon*, namely, " That a day cannot " be fixed for the trial of a Prifoner, in a ca- " pital cafe, in his abfence," feem to have been both infringed in the prefent cafe

2 Str. 825.

If I am told that the Prifoner here was prefent in *intendment* of law, I fay that will never fatisfy the law, intendments or legal fictions will not anfwer in fuch a caufe, he could not have been admitted to plead *de novo*, without a new arraignment, and having been *actually* prefent, and the cafe in *Strange* obvioufly applies to an *actual* and not a *legal* prefence in Court

82 3.

My next objection is that the *Venire* in this cafe was made returnable on an improper day, it was tefted on the 21ft of June, and returnable on the 16th of November, on a day *certain*, and not on a *common* return-day—And *Tuchin's* cafe, and *Layer's* cafe feem to be authorities in point to fhew that this is a fatal error, for here again I contend, that the day in which a Writ is made returnable

6 Mod 218

6 St. Tr.

is matter of law, and not of practice —Will any
one deny that it would be error, if there were
not fifteen days between the Teste and the Return of the *Venne*, and yet it might as well be
agreed that this was matter of practice merely,
as that the day on which a Writ is made returnable, is so

My next objection is that the severance of the
pannel in this case and by this Court, was unwarranted in point of law

The Court of King's Bench sitting over a matter which arose within its own proper county,
is undoubtedly a Court of General Gaol Delivery, but sitting upon a matter which arose in a
foreign county, and was removed into that Court
by *Certiorari*, I do assert, however absurd it may
seem, that it neither is, nor can be considered
as a Court of Gaol Delivery   See how this
Court is to proceed on a foreign case If the party be at large a *Capi..* issues, if he be in custody
an *Habeas Corpus* to bring him up and there
must be fifteen days between the *Teste* and *Return* of every Process that issues —Yet, if this
Court, in such a case, sat as a Court of General
Delivery, there would be no necessity in point of
law for such a slow and solemn mode of proceeding —Could this Court proceed on the sixteenth of November to try *Robert Keon*, on a
Jury returned immediately by the Sheriff of the
county of *Leitrim?* —Certainly not—And yet, if
this Court sat as a Court of Gaol Delivery on that
day, it clearly might have so proceeded

This Court sitting upon a matter which arises
in a foreign county, and is removed by *Certiorari*, proceeds by *Writ* Commissioners of *Oyer*
and *Terminer* proceed by *Precept*, which must
have fifteen days between its Teste and Return
but commissions of Gaol Delivery may and usually
do,

Rex
verfus
Keon.

do, proceed by *award* made *ore tenus*, and returnable *immediately* , and therefore this laft Court, and it alone, is competent to *fever* a pannel.

Let us fee what the fevering of the pannel is —Severing the pannel feems to be making that Jury, which was returned to try two or more perfons jointly, ferve as the Jury to try one of them fingly And thus Lord Chief Juft. *Kelyng* feems to underftand the phrafe. Now how is this to be done ? Why by quafhing as it were the *joint* Award and Return, and making a new Award, and caufing the Sheriff to make a new and immediate return of the firft pannel for the trial of the one prifoner only Now that fuch is the intendment of law, fee the words of Lord Chief Juftice *Kelyng* :——" That if feveral pri-
" foners be put upon one Jury, and they
" challenge peremptorily, and fever in their
" challenges, he who is challenged by one is to
" be drawn againft all, becaufe the pannel be-
" ing joint, one Juror cannot be drawn againft
" one, and fever for another.—But in fuch cafe
" it was agreed, the pannel might be fevered,
" *and that the Jury might be returned betwixt the*
" *King* and EVERY ONE of the prifoners—And
" THEN *when the Jury has been fo returned*,
" they (that is the prifoners) are to be tried
" *feverally, &c.*"

Kel 8 Ref.
P. 9.
Plowd.
100.
Hawk.
407. ch 41.
Sect 9.

Kelyng's
Rep pa.9.

If then I am right in my idea as to what the feverance of a pannel is, the power of fevering it muft be incidental merely to a Court proceeding by award, which may be returned *immediately* , and cannot be exercifed by a Court bound as this Court was in the prefent cafe, to proceed by Writ, having fifteen days between its Tefte and Return.

Lord

Earlsfort, C. J. — Is your argument that the Court of King's Bench is circumscribed in their power, and are more narrowed than the Court of Gaol Delivery at the Assizes ?—I do not understand you.

Mr. *Smith* —My argument is, that this Court sitting on a foreign matter removed hither by *Certiorari*, cannot award a Jury process returnable *immediately*, as a Court of general gaol delivery may, and consequently cannot sever a Jury pannel, according to my idea and definition of such severance

These, my Lords, are the grounds on which, in my poor opinion, the judgment in the present case ought to be arrested. But should your Lordships be inclined to a contrary opinion, I trust that you will at least respite execution, so as to give the Prisoner time to apply for a Writ of Error, in order to have these questions solemnly discussed and decided by the Judges of the land in the *dernier resort*.

Court —Remand the prisoner, and let him be brought up to-morrow.

Rex
versus
Keon,

Q   SATURDAY,

SATURDAY, JANUARY 26th. *B. R.*

IN purſuance of the laſt order, Robert Keon
was again brought up

Mr *Curran*—I am Counſel for the Crown in
this caſe, and when I conſider that the fate of
the Priſoner perhaps is now ultimately to be decided by the Court, and when I reflect upon the
neceſſity to which the law is reduced, of puniſh-
ing great offences with great ſeverity, it is ſome
conſolation to us who are concerned as Counſel
for the Crown, in our humble ſituation to feel
in common with the Court, that it is a blow
falling on the guilty for the protection of the
innocent.

When the Officer of your Court ſays, " God
" ſend you a good deliverance," it is a hu-
mane, and a pious wiſh, that the innocence
of the accuſed may be manifeſted, not that
his guilt ſhould eſcape with impunity. That
is now over The Jury have found the Priſoner
guilty of the charge. The evidence they went
on is now not a matter for Counſel to obſerve
on, and the judgment is now ſought to be ar-
reſted, not by any appeal to your compaſſion,
but on mere matters of law

The objections have been leſſening, in point
of number, as they advanced in the progreſs of
the motion, and I fear that while they decreaſed
in number, they do not increaſe in weight

The laſt Council promiſed to confine himſelf
to thoſe only which are tenible.

He

He confined his objections to the mif-return of the *Certiorari* only, as not being agreeable to the Mandate, that it was not on a proper day In anfwer to this, will the Court permit me to read the *Certiorari*? It is directed to two perfons who are perfectly diftinct, it had been truly ftated, that if the *Certiorari* be returned by an improper perfon, nothing is returned. *Afhley*'s cafe which is quoted to fupport the objection, is a cafe to fuftain this *Certiorari*, it is " *vos vel* " *aliquis veftrum*" The Return made by the Clerk of the Crown, is made by a known officer of the Crown, the whole objection depends on a fingle letter; if it had been the feals of you, or the feal of any of you, the objection could have no colour, and the fenfe is the fame. If there be any imperfection in this fingle letter, it might be amended even now, as in the *King* and *Atkinfon*, and even *a fortiori*, for in that cafe it was determined that the Return of the *Certiorari* was good even without a feal

In order to fhew that it was not returnable on a proper day, it was argued that it was an original Writ There is no queftion that proceedings may be returned into this Court by original from Chancery; then the original Writ in the name of the King is purchafed out of the *Officina Brevium*, the judicial Writ, as here, is tefted by the Chief Juftice; the one is to be purchafed, the other is not.

It is faid to be *quafi*, an original Writ, and the cafe of *Tuchin* and *Layer* were cited, but it muft be admitted where it iffues out of your own Court, you may return it when you pleafe

To fhew that it was not an original Writ, I fhall fhew the general nature of the return of Writs

Rex verfus Keon

Salk ub fup

Tit Cert. Dogherty C. C Affi.

*6 Mod ub fup.
6 St Tr. ub fub*

Q 2

Before

Rex
verfus
Keon.

Reeves's
Hift Com.
Law.

Com. Dig.

52 Hen
III.

Reeves,
paffim

F N B
Lilly's
Ent

Toft 347.

Before the divifion of the *Aula Regis*, all the year was term. Reeves fays that the divifion was partly neceffity, partly religion, fo Doddridge fays in Commyns, fo fays Blackftone

The firft trace of the *Dies in Banco* is to be found in the ftatute of Henry III there you will find the ftatute to be confined to civil cafes.

The King's Bench had an original, inherent right in criminal cafes, and of neceffity muft have had a power of making its own Writ returnable when it thought proper.

In fact, the Return was originally founded on the expediency and neceffity of the times. If it requires difpatch, you will make the Return *fine dilatione*, if not fo urgent, you will confider whether the party to whom it is directed, refides in the county of *Dublin*, or the county of *Antrim*. The day of Return in the King's Bench at Weftminfter, was determined by the diftance. Accordingly on indictments in the county where they fit, the Procefs is returnable immediately; on foreign indictments there are fifteen days between the Tefte and Return, but in Writs of *Certiorari* the return of them requires difpatch, and every original Chancery *Certioraris* were returnable *fine dilatione*.

The Court of King's Bench interferes in directing the practice, and has an original power of making the practice of their Court.

Until the reign of Edward III. the principals in the fecond degree could not be tried, till trial or outlawry of principal in the firft. If they fay the practice is the law, then what is the confequence?—They admit that this Court can alter the law, which is a pofition that I will not grant, although I contend that it can alter the practice; other-

otherwife the Court of King's Bench muft be a flave to the rules of practice broached by their predeceffors

If *Weftminfter* Hall then may make new practice, why not this Court.

Layer's cafe and *Tuchin*'s have been cited as to the Return, being a matter of law or matter of practice; as to that, the *Venire* in *Layer*'s cafe was on a common return day, and he ought to be tried, by the rule contended for, on the *quarto die poft* If that day be the day immediately after the three days which our fturdy anceftors required, it was not upon that day, if it meant four natural days, then it was not that day The Return was the 29th, and he was tried on the 21ft.

Layer's cafe is cited to fhew that it is error if the *Venire* be not returned on a common return day. But what did the Court do there, when it wanted to know the Rule? they called on Mr. *Harcourt* the Officer, who ftated what the *courfe* of the Court was, and Mr. *Harcourt* fupports his idea of a mere matter of practice, by a palpable miftake in matter of law

If your Jury Procefs be not continued, there is a chafm If you iffue no *diftringas* on return of the *Venire* they may go about their bufinefs; to keep them here you muft make the link complete

What a *difcontinuance* is, is matter of LAW.

What the *Return* of a Writ is, is matter of PRACTICE

It is faid that a *Certiorari* muft be returned on a common return day So it muft when iffuing out of Chancery. Why? That it fhall not be in the power of the Clerks in Chancery to compel the fubject to come at a time, when they

to

Rex
versus
Keon

know he cannot come. It is said there is an analogy between the *Certiorari* of this Court, and that of Chancery, and the same rules ought to be followed. It might be so, if there were no other method of bringing in the Record, but the Justices may bring in the Record *proprius manibus* when it is for the Crown.

2 Hale.

In criminal cases generally the Crown has the advantage of the party; and the rules of proceeding on the Crown side of the Court are more in favour of the Crown, for the furtherance of justice, by the facility of prosecution.

2 Hale,
210
2 Hale,
260.

It has been said that a *Certiorari* is a process on the indictment. It is not. The *Venire* is the first process, and Layer's Case as far as it goes, shews the *Return* of it to be mere matter of practice, for how was it settled there?—Upon the certificate of the Clerks.

The Queen and *Tuchin* differs much from the present Case, that was an information for a libel, and in that case there was an original writ of the Court.

It is said that when you sit in the county where the offence is committed, you are Judges of Gaol Delivery—but not otherwise —It would be strange to say, you will remove the Record from the Court of Gaol Delivery at the Assizes, if that Court has greater power to try it than yourselves—or that the more emanation from your Court should possess greater power than the source whence 'tis derived.

9 Rep.
119

It is laid down in *Sanchar's* case, generally that the Justices of this Court are the sovereign Judges of Gaol Delivery. And I contend that all the powers of the Judges of Gaol Delivery below, are at once *merged* in this Court by the *Certiorari*

You

You cannot award a *Venire immediate* on a foreign indictment, but that is the only difference between foreign and other indictments

Let me ask what the practice of this Court has been ?—But if the practice were not with us, would it be an authority to arrest the judgment Certainly not.—In *Layer*'s case the Judges said, they believed it had been both ways. A mere deviation from practice is not error for which a judgment can be arrested.

It is contended on the authority of an anomalous case, that the prisoner ought to plead *de novo*; and the Recorder says there was no issue But the case he cites says otherwise.—If there were no issue returned he could not waive it —— But it is asserted that he ought to be admitted to waive his plea ———Did he ask to waive it '

He ought to be allowed to plead to the jurisdiction.—But it is a Rule of law, that after pleading in chief no man shall be assisted to plead a *dilatory* plea, and that was the opinion of the Court in *Layer*'s case.

Suppose you arraigned him here again, and he stood mute ——Could you find him standing *mute* of *malice*, when it already appeared upon your Record that he had pleaded

It is said upon the authority of the *King* and *Johnson*, that he ought to be present when his trial was fixed What is notice of trial on circuit ?——The being in prison If it were not every prisoner ought to have notice of the coming of the Judge. And though no Indictment be yet found against the Prisoner, yet his being in prison is sufficient notice of trial Here the issue joined, was the foundation for the award of process

proceſs to try it, and for that his preſence was utterly immaterial

He applied by his Counſel not to be removed on account of his inability, and that is now endeavoured to be made a ground of error

Having now gone through almoſt all of the objections, I come to the laſt point, the ſevering the *Venire* And I confeſs, that had I any wiſh to ſave the Priſoner, I ſhould be hopeleſs when I come to that.

I admit that when the Proceſs is one joint Proceſs, it cannot afterwards be ſeveral; and that where the *Venire* is joint the *Diſtringas* muſt be ſo likewiſe.——But it was upon the *Venire* he was tried

I admit Mr. Smith's definition of the *Venire* to be perfectly right, and in ſpeaking to this ſubject, I ſhall endeavour rather to apply myſelf to known principle, than to the authority of a *ſolitary* caſe

1ſt. Then the offences were ſeveral, and there was therefore no illegality in having them tried ſeverally.——If there be any right to be tried jointly, it muſt be an original right that co-offenders have to avail themſelves of. In the caſe
4 St Tr. of *Cranbourn* and *Rookwood*, the *Venires* were ſeparate, though the offence was joint.

It is ſaid that Judges of Gaol Delivery may ſever a pannel, and award a *Tales*, that is a *dictum*, upon which I ſhall preſently make ſome obſervations, and the reaſon alledged, why they can do it, is becauſe the Award is only verbal.

In *Saliſbury's* caſe the Court does not ſeem to
Saliſburys Caſe.
Plowden 100. have acted as judges of gaol-delivery; but you do not here act as ſuch. They awarded a *tales* which they could not do as a court of gaol-delivery.

It

It was a joint procefs, and alfo a *tales* on that procefs. By the *common law* the Prifoner had a right to five and thirty peremptory challenges; by *Statute*, they were reduced to twenty only. The Crown had a right to challenge the whole pannel as *non boni pro Rege*, and was not bound to fhew caufe until the whole pannel is gone through. The Statute does not fay when; but the Court has always conftrued it in favour of the Crown. If the analogy had been followed, the Crown muft have fhewn caufe prefently — Four other perfons had a right to twenty peremptory challenges: if they concur, they had a right to make eighty challenges; and a cafe in the Year-books may be cited, but what was that? It was a cafe of appeal.

It is contended, why fhould Mr. *Keon* be deprived of this peremptory challenge?—Why fhould he not have the benefit of *their* challenges? I anfwer, becaufe the ftatute gives him no more than twenty.

Hawkins is cited on this occafion, as is *Hale*, who fay, anciently juftices (not of gaol-delivery) might fever the pannel, but *Fofter* has charged *Hale*, on this occafion, with confounding indictment and appeal; the latter of which is an unfavoured action, whofe practice cannot be held out as fimilar to the proceeding by indictment, which is a favoured profecution

There are five perfons in the dock. They will not join in their challenges—perhaps becaufe they want to opprefs their co-indictor. You will fever them, why?—becaufe fhould you admit them to join, it may be an injury rather than a benefit to him.

Suppofe one of them out on bail, fuppofe one of them dies, fuppofe one of them does not ap-

R   pear;

pear, fuppofe one of them runs mad, fhall the
juftice of the land be defeated, and no trial ever
be had? If not, there is no neceffity that the
trial fhould be joint. On the contrary, the arraignment and plea is feveral, fo may the verdict be totally different, and of courfe fo may
the judgment, and by a parity of reafoning fo
may the trials

Thus far I have argued this point on principle
only, and if it wants the authority of any cafe,
I have one, which I fhall quote to your Lordfhips, and for which I am indebted to the induftry of a learned gentleman near me, (Mr.
Williams). But it is a cafe which fquares with
every part of the prefent point, it is the cafe of
Dyer 151 *Thymolby* and *Gray*, in Dyer.—There three of
the jury were actually fworn and charged with
two prifoners; and there the prifoners not join-
ing in their challenge, the pannel, or rather the
trial was fevered, and the party tried found
guilty.

Court—Remand the Prifoner till further orders.

TUESDAY, JANUARY 29, 1788. *B. R*

By the Court —Let Robert Keon be brought up
on Thurfday next.

THURSDAY, JANUARY 31, 1788. *B. R.*

Robert Keon was brought up, according to the
order of Tuefday laft, and the Court proceeded
feriatim, to give their reafon for refufing to arreft
the judgment

Earlsfort, C J —This was an Indictment found
at Lent Affizes 1787, in the county of Leitrim,
againft Robert Keon, Ambrofe Keon, Edward
Keon,

Keon, Patrick Carty, and Michael Mullarky, for the murder of George Nugent Reynolds, on the 16th of October, 1786; and the import of the Indictment is, that the said Robert Keon gave to the said George Reynolds one mortal wound on his forehead, by firing a shot from a pistol and that the rest of the persons in the Indictment were present, comforting, abetting and assisting, contrary to the statute by which *Murder* is *deemed* HIGH TREASON in Ireland, and punished as such.

Rex versus Keon.

10 Hen. 7

The first time this case was mentioned in this Court was on the 19th of May, in Easter Term last, when Mr Attorney General suggested some improper conduct at the Assizes, the freeholders refusing to answer their names, by which the trials were necessarily put off by the Judges of Assize, and prayed a *Certiorari* to remove the Indictment into this Court, which was granted.

On the 16th of June, in Trinity Term last, he also moved for a *Habeas Corpus* to remove the bodies of the Prisoners, which was also granted.

On the 23d of June, in the same Term, Mr Prime Serjeant, by licence, on behalf of Robert Keon, and Mr. Smith on behalf of Ambrose Keon, moved the Court to remand the Record, and grounded their motion on affidavits of the ill health of the Prisoners As a motive for granting this application, they urged that there could be a more speedy trial below. This motion was opposed by the Attorney General, and there appearing a diversity of statements on the affidavits, as to the health of the Prisoners, this motion was refused

The Record was then in Court, and we were all of opinion, that in order to have any trial whatsoever, it would be better to have it at the bar of this Court. On this last motion there was

R 2

no

no objection whatſoever made to the *Certiorari*; nor any ſuggeſtion that the Record was not well removed, though that would have determined the motion in favour of the Priſoner   On the contrary, the motion made by the Priſoner's Counſel, to remand the Record, admitted it to be in Court

On the 27th day of June a day was pre-fixed for the trial on the motion of Mr. Geoghegan.

On the 16th day of November, the day prefixed, the Priſoners were brought up, and two hundred and forty-two Jurors appearing, they were aſked if they would join in their challenges, which being refuſed by them, the Court determined to try Robert Keon alone

As ſoon as the pannel was called over, Robert Keon made an affidavit to poſtpone his trial, and one of the reaſons aſſigned was, that there was too great a number of perſons on it   Here again he had an opportunity of objecting to the *Certiorari*, or indeed to the return of the *Venire*, but no ſuch objection was made.

The Priſoner then challenged the array, and his cauſes of challenge were, that there was too great a number of Jurors returned, and that the Sheriff in his Return of the execution of the *Venire* ſaid, " as may appear by the *pannels* an-nexed", in the plural number

To this challenge the Counſel for the Crown *demurred*, and the Priſoner's Counſel having *joined* in demurrer, the challenge was over-ruled.

It appeared by the Record certified unto this Court, that Robert and the others had been ar-raigned and pleaded ſeparately at the Aſſizes, and that iſſue had been then joined.

When

When his arraignment and plea were read to him by the Clerk of the Crown in the King's Bench, he ſignified no deſire, nor did his Counſel apply for leave to withdraw that plea, and this having been the antient, univerſal practice of the Court, he was given in charge to the Jury upon his former arraignment and plea of Not Guilty, ſo repeated to him, upon that iſſue ſo joined below, and having challenged twenty of the Jurors peremptorily, and ſome others upon cauſe ſhewn, he was, after the examination of ſeveral witneſſes on both ſides, convicted

After four days he was brought up to receive judgment, and his Counſel made ſeveral objections for the purpoſe of arreſting it, and that he and his Counſel may be ſatisfied that wherever the Court could bend in lenity they did, I ſhall obſerve, that theſe objections were not made to the *Indictment*, but to the *Jury Proceſs* and *Mode* of Trial

The firſt claſs of objections are to the *Certiorari*.

1. That it was miſ-directed.
2. That it was miſ returned.
3. That it was not returned on a *day in Bank.*

As to the two firſt, the mere reading of the *Certiorari* anſwers them, [Here his Lordſhip read the *Certiorari* and Return] it would be an idle waſte of time to go farther into this part of the objections, as the Return actually indents with the command of the Writ. Ante Pa. 12

The third objection is, that the *Certiorari* is an *original Writ.* An *original* Writ iſſuing out of Chancery is teſted by the King himſelf, a *judicial* Writ is a Writ of this Court, under its ſeal, and is teſted by the Chief Juſtice only   It is contended that it ought to be made returnable on a day in Bank, that is not the fact—In the caſe of *Shaen* and the Earl of *Kildare*, the *Certiorari* was returned by Sir *John Pine*, and was a Re- turn Lilly Ent 560.

turn *immediate* So was the cafe of *Murray* of *Broughton*, and fo it muft be from the nature and office of the Writ, as being to ftop all proceedings below. Having faid thus much to thefe objections to the *Certiorari*, I fhall take leave of them, as neither founded in *fact*, *practice*, or *principle*

The next objection was, that the *Habeas Corpus* is another *original* Writ, and alfo to be returned on a common return day, if the reafoning as to the *Certiorari* be founded—*A fortiori*, it goes to the *Habeas Corpus* It was objected that the *Habeas Corpus* was returned the laft day of Term, and that this was Error; but a *Habeas Corpus* is returnable in vacation, as well as in term time; at the Judges Chambers as well as in Court, and the fooner this conftitutional Writ is returnable the better. This clafs of objections was very properly deferted as foon as made

The *Venire* was then objected to, and thefe objections feem to go farther than the reft, and I fhall therefore pay them more attention than the others, and they are,

1. That the *Venire* was awarded and tefted before the Prifoner was at the bar of the Court.

2. That it was not properly returned, being returned on a day *certain*, and not on a day *in bank*.

3 That the *Venire* was *joint*, and the trial of the Prifoner was *feveral*

Under the firft objection it is contended, that there was fuch a *chafm* as creates a *difcontinuance*; but the Tefte of the *Venire* anfwers that—The *Habeas Corpus* was tefted the twenty-feventh of June, and the *Venire* is tefted the fame day. Here is no *chafm*

It is faid, and truly, that the *Venire* is returnable on the fixteenth of November, Friday next after the Morrow of Saint Martin, which is neither a general return day, nor the *quarto die poft*, *poſt*, and an expreſſion of Lord Chief Juſtice Pratt in *Layer*'s Caſe, is urged as ſupporting the objection, this however is only a point of *practice*, in which both kingdoms differ. I would here diſtinguiſh between legal fictions, adopted for the attainment of Juſtice, and general Rules of Courts, which are regulations for that purpoſe, ſometimes the ſame in all Courts, ſometimes different, though upon the ſame circumſtances, which are called the practice of the Court, and thoſe common and ſtatute law, right and preſcriptions, which are above the power of Judges to vary. In Great Britain the *practice* is, that the *Venue* is returnable on a *common day*; in Ireland on a *common day*, or a *day certain*, as it ſuits the diſcretion of the Court.

Rex verſus Keon 6 St. Tr.

The *practice* of the Court is the *law* of the Court, and muſt not be varied with the occaſion, eſpecially in criminal caſes; that the Priſoner may not have it to ſay, "I have not been dealt equally with, there has been a variance in the rules of the Court as to me.

That the practice of the Court is equal to the common law right, is determined in the caſe of *Layer*, elſe why refer to the officer, Mr *Harcourt*, who upon that occaſion ſays, "I ſhall be very tender in this affair, when the life of a man is concerned, and will not ſay any thing but what I am ſure is the *courſe* of the Court." This ſurely evinces the poſition, that the practice of the Court is the law of the Court, elſe why refer to the officer?

6 St. Tr 329.

In order to inform ourſelves of what had been the antient and univerſal practice in this kingdom, we directed our officer, not depending upon his mere report (as in *Layer*'s caſe) to make ſearch for precedents, and he has accordingly certified to us all the *Ventres* for twenty-ſeven years back, and they all appear to be made returnable upon a day *certain*, regardleſs of the days

days *in bank*, it might happen otherwife; but from the practice there appears no neceffity for it, nor was it ever objected to, though Writs of Error lay to Great Britain until within the laft five years And fuppofe a Writ of Error brought, what would the Lords in England do? They would act as they formerly did, (in a poffeffory cafe, where the decree of Lord *Lifford* was appealed from) and direct the practice to be certified to them, and they would determine according to the practice.

During the period certified to us, there have been no lefs than forty-three trials at the bar of this Court, and the Hall never was more ably fupplied by profeffional men than during that period, and all thefe judgments were acquiefced in, and appear to have been the uniform practice, and this I am confirmed in, as fome of the Judges of this Court, when I came to the Bench, had prefided in it for the laft thirty years, and if the practice were to be fettled this day, I do not know that I fhould prefer the practice in England, except from my wifh to keep the practice and the law in both countries as near to each other as may be.

Every reafon, which is given in the books, for a *common return* day, or for the *quarto die poft*, has vanifhed. That the fturdy Englifhman fhould not attend when called upon, is no longer any thing like common fenfe I do not mean to cenfure the practice in *Weftminfter* Hall, I only fay I can fee no reafon for varying the practice from what I have found it to have been for thirty years paft

The practice, it is admitted, in England is to make the Writ returnable within fifteen days, as a fpace of time fufficient for coming from one extremity of England to another, here there were almoft five months not only for the Jury, but for the Prifoner.

But

But it is objected that the Prisoner should have been present at the appointment of his trial, he was virtually present by his Counsel. That it should be error that he was not then present, is extraordinary—Was he not in the custody of this Court from the Return of the *Habeas Corpus?* Besides, he made no objection of this fort upon his trial, nor could he, for there was nothing like hardship dealt to him; for his Counsel stated his ill state of health, and it was lenity to suffer him to come up at his leisure.

Rex *versus* Keon.

It is objected by his Counsel, that he was not arraigned or put to plead here. To support this doctrine, the cases cited are peculiarly unfortunate Can a man who had not pleaded, apply to withdraw his plea? Surely this alone shews that he had pleaded. If he were admitted to plead again, there would have been perhaps two inconsistent pleas upon the Record, unless he had withdrawn the former.

The next objection is to the number of the Jury upon the pannel, as being against the spirit of the statute of *Edward* the first, this was over-ruled in *Layer's* case, and in many other cases. In this Court in the case of the *King* and *Sheehy*, which was tried before my Lord *Annally* and my brother *Henn*, there were sixty Jurors. And this seems consonant with the reasoning of my Lord *Hale*, in his History of the Common Law, that there may be as many unexceptionable Jurors as possible, in order to be certain that there may be a sufficient number of proper persons on the Jury.

P. 286

The last objection is to the severance of the pannel, and as to that I shall be more particular, because that was an act of the Court—And I shall shew that the severing of the pannel, or rather the severing of the trial was founded.

S   1st, On

Rex
v. pl.
Keon.

1ft, On principle

2d, On the authority of cafes   And

3d, In practice.

That this is a Court of Supreme Criminal
Jurifdiction, *Oyer* and *Termine*, and *Gaol De-
livery*, may be collected *Sparfim* from *Hale* and
Hawkins The Judges of this Court are the
Sovereign Judges of *Gaol Delivery* and *Oyer and
Terminer*, you will find in a note to the new

*Note to
p 11*

edition of HAWKINS by LEACH, a book dedi-
cated to the prefent Chief Baron *Eyre* It is faid
there that when one " Jury is jointly returned
" for the trial of feveral defendants before Juf-
" tices of *gaol delivery*, it is certain they may
" afterwards fever the pannel if they find it ex-
" pedient."

*2 Hawk
cap 4
fect 9 p
57 —4
new Ed
p   old
Ld.p.407*

It is admitted that this Court is the Supreme
Court, and poffeffes the power of a Court of Gaol
Delivery, and fhall not this Court be permitted to
do that which it is acknowledged the inferior Court
can do? Is this Court to be circumfcribed by
the *Venire*, and not do that which it is admitted on all hands it could do if it were in the
county where the fact happened.

The only found difference between a trial at
the bar of the Court by *Venire*, and at the Affizes is, that in the firft of thefe cafes there fhall be
fifteen days between the Tefte and Return of the
Writ, in the other the Jury Precept iffues *inftanter* Both Rules are founded in convenience.
In the one, that the Jury may have time when
they are to go to a remote diftance, whereas in the
other the whole of the county is fuppofed to be
prefent

The cafes cited from *Hale* and *Hawkins* feem
only to go to Appeal

This Court was not unapprized of the cafe
which was cited by Mr *Curran* at the Bar, it
was firft furnifhed me by the induftry of my
Brother

Brother *Bennett*, and it meets every part of the
cafe, finding however, fome *dictums* made use
of to the contrary, I availed myfelf of the affiftance of the firft abilities in thefe kingdoms,
and I fhall here read what Lord *Mansfield* has
faid, as to the two queftions which I put to his
Lordfhip, and what thefe queftions were, will
appear by his Lordfhip's letter

Dyer 152.
Dalifor
— p 11
Benl — 7.
Moore 12.
Co Lit
155 —6.

" I took the moft fatisfactory way of anfwer-
" ing your Lordfhip's two queftions

" All the Judges were confulted upon them,
" and we are *all* of opinion as follows ——As
" to the firft queftion——That it would be error in
" *Weftminfter Hall*, if a trial for murder were
" had upon the day that the *Venire* was actu-
" ally returned, unlefs it were upon a *general*
" *return-day* In other words the *Venire* upon
" an Indictment in *Weftminfter Hall*, muft be
" returnable on a general return day; but for
" the fame reafon, on which we found this
" opinion, we think it is not error in *Ireland* —
" In the King's Bench in *England*, the conftant
" and invariable practice has been, to make the
" *Venire* returnable on a *General Return-day*.
" But in *Ireland* the antient and conftant prac-
" tice is *ftated* to have been to make it returna-
" ble on a *day certain*, we think that in this in-
" ftance the *Practice makes the law*, and it is to
" cafes like the prefent that the maxim *Com-*
" *munis Error facit jus*, peculiarly applies
 As to the Second Queftion
" We think it would not be error if the prin-
" cipal in the firft degree alone, were tried in
" confequence of the *Venire's* being a joint one
" The Indictment in its nature is *joint* and *fe-*
" *veral*, and notwithstanding the feveral Pleas
" of the Prifoners will warrant a joint *Venire*,
" if at the trial the Prifoners *joined* in their

" Challenges;

" Challenger, they might be tried *jointly*, but if
" they *fever* in their challenges, the *Courfe* has
" been to try them *feverally*, on account of the
" difficulty of getting a Jury after all the Chal-
" lenges to try them *jointly*."

I have thus endeavoured to anfwer the feveral objections that have been made, and I am
now to pronounce my opinion, in which we
are all unanimous, that the judgment ought not
to be arrefted.

Henn, J.—The *firft objection* that was relied on
was that the *Certiorari* was mif-returned.

The clear anfwer to that is the *direction*, and
the *mandatory* part of the writ.

It was returned by the Clerk of the Crown,
under his feal, in whofe cuftody the Record was,
and to whom it was directed.

Salk 479
Eliz Afbley's cafe, which was cited, the Return
was by the Clerk of the Peace, to whom it was
not directed, but to two Juftices.

The *fecond objection* was, that both the *Certiorari*
and *Venire Facias* ought to have been returnable on
a *general return day*, and not on a *day certain*.

The Anfwer to this is, that as to *Certioraris*
iffued out of Chancery, they are generally made
returnable without delay, without naming either
a *general* return-day or a day certain

If iffued out of this Court, both with refpect
to *Certioraris* and *Venire Facias*, as they are both
judicial writs, they are to be made returnable, according to the *uniform* and *eftablifhed practice* of
the Court, and that is upon a day certain.

We have been furnifhed with precedents for feven and twenty years paft, and they are all made
returnable on a day certain

From hence I think this inference neceffarily
follows, that the practice and rule of this Court
has been uniformly and conftantly fo.   If fo, this
practice

practice then stands confirmed by the statute relative to appointing days in bank, in which
there is this proviso—"That in such cases as spe-
" cial days have used to be given for returning of
" writs and processes, it shall be lawful for the Jus-
" tices of every of the Courts of Records, in all
" the processes by them to be awarded, to assign
" special days of returns, as by their discretions
" shall be thought convenient."

With respect to the rule and practice laid down
in *Layer's* Case, that the *Venire* is to be made returnable on a general return-day, though in fact
the Jury is not to appear, nor the trial be had,
'till the *quarto die post*, it probably is not the
practice now in England; for in all the precedents of *Venire Facias* laid down in *Lilly's Entries*,
they are all made returnable in a day certain,
exactly agreeable to our practice.

But admitting the practice to be still the same in
England, it would only prove that the practice in
the two kingdoms differs; and I will be bold to
assert, that our practice is more consonant to sound
sense and reason than theirs, for their practice
manifestly tends to mislead the Jury, by appointing one day for their appearing to try, when,
in fact, the trial is not to be 'till three or four
days after, whereas, by our mode, the Jury
know to a certainty the day on which they are
to appear, and the trial is to proceed. I therefore
think there is no weight in that objection.

It was objected, that the *Prisoner* ought to have
been present when his trial was appointed.

In my apprehension he was not, in law, intitled to be present, it is mere matter of indulgence.

I take the distinction to be that, if a prisoner before conviction has any thing to move,
he may do it by his Counsel or Agent, but need
not be present, but after conviction, if he wants

to

Marginal notes:

Rex *versus* Keon.

6 Geo I. cap 1 s. 10.

6 St. Tr. ub. sup.

675.

Rex
verfus
Keon.

2 Str 84,
368 1227
to move any thing as in arreft of judgment, or for a new trial, he muft be brought up to Court, not out of favour, but for fecuring the prifoner after he is convicted And this feems to me clear from the cafes cited by Mr Caldbeck

It was next objected, that when the Prifoner was brought up, he ought to have been arraigned here, with liberty to withdraw his plea below, and to plead *de novo* In fupport of which, was cited, the *King* againft *Baker*, and the *King* againft *Carpenter*

Carth. 6
4 Vin.
Ab 362
p. .

I would firft obferve, that the cafes cited are of mifdemeanors, in which greater incuigence may be given , but not a fingle cafe was cited, nor, do I believe, was to be found, where it was ever done in a capital cafe It might be attended with the moft dangerous confequences if fuch dilatories were to be admitted in capital cafes.

Befides, if fuch indulgences were at all admiffible, it certainly ought to have been in confequence of fome fpecial application made by the Prifoner for that purpofe, antecedent to the trial , and this, I think, is clearly to be inferred Carth 6. from the Cafe of the *King* and *Boker*. For, in my apprehenfion, it would be abfurd to fay, that after iffue was regularly joined below, and returned here, that it was incumbent on this Court *de jure* to arraign the Prifoner again, without his confent , for otherwife, *non conflat*, that the prifoner either wifhed or defired it

No fuch application was made in the prefent Cafe.

But what I principally rely on as an anfwer to thofe objections is, that by the Prifoner's coming to the bar, and praying *oyer* of the Indictment, and afterwards *challenging* the *array* of the pannel was, in my apprehenfion, to be confidered in law as a clear admiffion that all the antecedent proceedings were right and regular,

and

and *salves* any antecedent irregularities, if any such there were, and therefore that the Prisoner now comes too late, after conviction, to urge any of those objections in arrest of judgment

In the Case of the *King* against *Rookwood* for High Treason, the defendant's counsel objected to the proceeding on the trial, insisting it ought to be postponed, in regard they had not a true and full copy of the indictment agreeable to the statute. But it was there said by the Court, you ought to have insisted upon this at the time of your arraignment, but as you have pleaded, you now *come too late, as it must be now taken for granted you had a sufficient copy to enable you to plead, as you did not object before you pleaded.*

This seems to me to be a strong authority in point.

The *last objection* was, that as the *Venire* was joint to try five prisoners on an indictment removed by *Certiorari* from a foreign county, that this Court was not authorised by law to fever the pannel for the trial of one prisoner only

It is admitted that this Court is the supreme Court of *Oyer* and *Terminer* and *Gaol-delivery*, and that they have all the powers of *Gaol-delivery* and *Oyer* and *Terminer* vested in them — It is admitted that Justices of *Gaol-delivery* have a power to fever the pannel when the prisoners refuse to join in their challenge

Can any one found reason be assigned why this Court shall not exercise a similar power on a similar occasion? It seems to carry an absurdity on the face it, to say that the inferior jurisdiction shall have greater power vested in them than the superior.

With respect to the distinction insisted on between an indictment found in the county where the King's Bench sits, and where found in a foreign county, makes no difference with respect to the present question. The only difference it makes

makes, is that where the indictment is of the
ſame county, a *Venire* may iſſue returnable immediately, or a bare award will be ſufficient for
returning a Jury, but where it is of a foreign
county, a *Venire* muſt iſſue, and there muſt be
fifteen days between the teſte and the return —
But it makes no difference with reſpect to the
power of the Court of ſevering the pannel. That
remains without any controul or reſtraint

It has been argued, that as the *Venire* is joint,
it cannot be *ſevered.*

If the law was ſo, this inconvenience would
neceſſarily follow, that all or none could be
tried. So that if one of the priſoners ſhould,
by ſickneſs, be unable to attend, or ſhould eſcape, none of the others ſhould be tried. What
an inconvenience and delay of juſtice this would
create muſt be obvious to every one!

But I conceive the law not to be ſo, but to be
thus ——

That a *Venire*, though joint againſt ſeveral, in
order that all may be tried at once, to ſave the
neceſſity of ſeveral trials, and that neceſſarily,
yet in point of law they are conſidered as ſeveral pannels, to try the ſeveral priſoners ſeparately, if made neceſſary by their refuſing to
join in their challenges

Upon this principle it was, that the trial in
Dyer 152. the Caſe of *Thymolby* againſt *Grey* was determined by the Courts of King's Bench and Com-
mon Pleas to be right. Which opinion ſtands
unimpeached by any author cited, or that I was
4 St Tr
663 able to diſcover. In the Caſe of the *King* againſt
Rookwood, it is ſaid there were ſeveral *Venire*
iſſued, why, to anſwer the convenience of the
Court, which had only a commiſſion of *Oyer* and
Terminer, and does not apply to the Court, and
2 Hawk.
141. ſ 9. the expreſſions of *Hawkins* are equally vague and
indefinite.

It

I therefore, upon the whole, am of opinion
that none of the objections urged by the Prifoner are, in law, fufficient to *arreft* the Judgment
in the prefent cafe.

Rex
verfus
Keon.

Bradftreet, J ——This being a cafe of confi-
derable expectation, I fhall mention thofe reafons which induce me to concur with the reft of
the Court in the decifion we are about to make.
Several objections have been made to the proceedings in this cafe

Firft, As to the *Certiorari*

1ft, That it was *mif-directed* —It is not fo.

2dly, That it was *mif-returned* —It is no fo.

3dly, That it was not returnable on a *general
return* day.

The fame objections are made to the *Venire*.

This appears to be not matter of *Law*, but of
Practice and *Regulation*.

In all the cafes where the *Law* is faid to be,
that there fhall be fifteen days between the tefte
and the return, there is no reftriction as to the
return day.

In *Layer's* cafe, the *Officer* of the Court was
applied to for information.

Firft *Shower* fhews it to be but matter of
practice, as it directs the firft return day of the
next term to be the day

336.

The practice here is different, as appears
from the Return made us of proceedings, of the
like nature, for feven and twenty years

But, even if the objection had any weight, it
is now too late to make it

Many defects, which at an early ftage of a
caufe may be taken advantage of, are cured by
appearance, and omitting to make the objection
in proper time.

T

The

Rex
verſus
Keon.
2 Hawk
301, 302.

The Defendant appearing ſhall not object to the Proceſs on which he has appeared, " *That it was not returnable on a proper day,* or that it *had not ſo many days as it ought between its Teſte and Return,*" or for any ſuch like defect

The reaſoning applies alike in the preſent inſtance

No objection was made on this ground by the Priſoner before or when he was brought to trial.

Beſides, ſhall he be allowed to make objections to the *Venire, after he has challenged the Return* to it, without objecting by his challenge to the *Venire* itſelf

By his challenge, he did not pray that the *Venire* ſhould be quaſhed, but only the *Return* by the Sheriff to it.

This, according to every idea of pleading, affirms the *Venire*

As to the objection that the Priſoner ſhould be arraigned in this Court, and plead *de novo,*

This is but matter of *Practice,* and not of *Right*

Nor is it laid down in any caſe to be the *Law.*

The caſes cited, only amount to ſhew that the Priſoner is *admitted* to plead *de novo, if he deſires it.*

If the Priſoner had any reaſon to offer for withdrawing the plea below, he might have ſhewn it, and probably he would have been admitted

However, he muſt have withdrawn the plea below, for what an abſurdity, nay *Error* would
follow,

follow, if two diftinct fubftantive pleas fhould appear on the Record.

The cafes quoted,

The *King* againft *Baker*, cannot be law in the latitude therein mentioned. Carth 6.

The *King* againft *Aylett*
The *King* againft *Shipley*.
The *King* againft *Ward*.

Thefe cafes only fhew that the *fuperior* Court does not look upon itfelf as bound by the proceedings of the *inferior* Court, if juftice and the Prifoner's cafe require that he fhould be permitted to withdraw his plea below, and plead here *de novo*.

Here, by his *Challenge* to the Array, he *affirms* his *Plea*

As to the objection that he was not *perfonally* prefent, when the day of his Trial was fixed,

He certainly, in *Intendment of Law*, was prefent.

In the *King* againft *Johnfon*, per Lord Raymond, it is faid to be a *Rule of the Court* in capital cafes never to move any thing in the abfence of the Defendant 2d Strange 625.

It feems to be a reafonable *Practice*, but furely a Prifoner may *waive* it

Quisque poteft renunciare Juri pro fe introducto

Might he not at any day in Michaelmas term laft *before*, or even *on the day of trial*, have defired another day if he thought proper

But if notice be neceffary to be given *in perfon* to prifoners of their day of trial, how can they have it from the Court in cafes to be tried at the Affizes in the country, which are but as

one

one day, and where every Prisoner is supposed in intendment of law be tried on the first
day.

The Commissions do not issue until too late
for such notice

They are not in force in the country until
opened, which is the first day, and *then* and not
before is there any intercourse between the Court
and the prisoners

Does it ever appear on the Record, that the
Prisoner is *present* when *the Venire* is awarded,

Except that immediately after issue joined, the
Venire is awarded.

Afterwards follows *a day to the Prisoner* and *for
the appearance of the Jury.*

This is to prevent a discontinuance, and but
legal fiction: And when the Record is made up,
all will appear as it ought

If any real inconvenience arose to the Prisoner from the appointment of the particular
day of Trial, the Court might have been informed of it, and probably would have fixed
it so as to induce no hardship upon the Prisoner.

It is now too late.

As to the last objection, which seems to be
the most plausible, namely, the *severing the
pannel* ,

It is agreed, that the Justices of *Gaol Delivery* may sever the pannel

It is agreed, that the *Judges of the King's-
Bench* are the supreme *Justices of Gaol Delivery*

But a distinction is taken as to the powers of
severing the pannel, which as to them, is to
be understood as relating to proceedings in the
Country

Country where they fit, and taken up by them there *originally*, and not to proceedings removed before them from a *foreign county*.

Rex ซเฟฟุ่ม Keon.

In what Law Book is this Reftriction laid down?

The only material reftriction feems to be, that of giving fifteen days between the Tefte and the Return of their own Writs of *Venire*, and this upon the ground of neceffity and convenience.

But when this rule of law is laid down is there any reftriction eftablished, as to their power of fevering the pannel?—None

If not, let us fee what Lord *Hale* fays—Before Juftices of *Gaol Delivery*, though at firft the award be *joint*, and the pannel *accordingly* returned, and the Prifoners challenge peremptorily *feverally*, whereby there are not left upon the pannel enough to try them, and a tales is awarded returnable the next day, and yet the Court, may even the next day, fever the firft award, and alfo the *Tales*.

2d Hale 264.

Salifbury's Cafe. Plow 100.

But it is faid, this is done by the *ordinary* Juftices of *Gaol Delivery*, becaufe they make an award *ore tenus*, and not by *Writ*, as the King's Bench does.

But though this be the ufual method, yet the Commiffioners of *Gaol Delivery may*, and in ftrictnefs *ought* to proceed by *Writ* or *Precept*.

For in Second *Hale*, where this is laid down, there is a precedent of a *Writ of Venire* from the Commiffioners of *Gaol Delivery* to the Sheriff, importing feveral matters, and in particular for the Return of a Jury

32, 33, 34

But

But although this folemnity of fummons, *may* and *fhould* be ufed, yet they *may* command the Sheriff *ore tenus*, to return a pannel without any Precept in *writing* to him.

So that no argument for the Prifoner's purpofe can be inferred from their ufual mode of proceedings by award *ore tenus*.

They may proceed by *Writ*, and if they do, I know no law which fays they may not fever the pannel, if they fee expedient.

Then it comes to this, whether this Court may not for the purpofes of juftice and expepiency, ufe *their* own Writ, as fuch Juftices do their Precept *ore tenus*.

It is faid a Tales confiftent with the *Venire*, could not have been granted, as it muft have been a *feveral* Tales, and the *Venire* was a joint one.

The inference is not true.

For the *Venire* upon the feverance of the pannel becomes feveral, and the Tales would correfpond

264.

And by the cafe in *Hole*, the Court of *Gaol Delivery* may after a joint award of the pannel, and a *joint* Tales, when the award is fevered, alfo *fever* the Tales to make them confiftent with each other.

The fevering the *Tales* can be done by the Juftices of *Gaol Delivery*, merely as being *alfo* Juftices of *Oyer* and *Terminer*, who always proceed by Writ or Precept in writing, and *only* can grant a *Tales*.

And yet, though proceeding by Precept in writing only, it appears the Tales which originates with them, may be fevered to make it agree with the feverance of the *joint* award by them as Commiffioners of Gaol Delivery

When

When it is confidered that all Commiffions whether of Oyer and Terminer, or of Gaol Delivery, proceed from the Crown, it feems a little extraordinary, that the King fhall have lefs power when he brings the Record to be tried *before himfelf*, than when he delegates his power to inferior characters of his own creating, namely ordinary Commiffioners of Gaol Delivery When the caufe is *removed*, this is a Court of *Gaol Delivery* to all Purpofes, except the fifteen days between the Tefte and Return.

Thus far I have confidered this point in the cafe upon principles.

But the Cafe of *Thymolby* and *Gray*, is in point; therefore I concur with his Lordfhip and my Brethren, that judgment ought not to be arrefted.

Bennett, J.——The reafons for refufing the prefent motion in arreft of judgment, have been fo fully ftated, and the objections made by the Prifoner's Counfel fo fully anfwered, that I fhall confine myfelf to a few obfervations on the cafes cited, and a few cafes in fupport of thofe obfervations.

It has been urged that the *Certiorari* ought to have been returnable on a general return-day— To fupport this they cite *Shower*.

In my opinion, a *Certiorari* iffuing out of this Court is a *judicial* and not an *original* Writ.—— Our Writ is tefted by the Chief Juftice—An original Writ iffues out of the Court of *Chancery*, and is tefted by the King himfelf.—I fpeak in general of original Writs, and perhaps the little intercourfe between the Crown and the Clerks

in

(margin) Rex verfus Keon. Dyer 152. b. 1 Shower 336.

in Chancery, made it neceffary to limit and appoint the Returns to certain fixed days —Our judicial Writs being immediately under the controul of the Court, required not this neceffity, and it was better to leave the term of them to the difcretion of the Court.

The reference in *Shower* contains a Latin rule made in the 3d year of William and Mary , it is not declaratory of the law , it looks forward, and upon examining it will be found to relate only to *Certioraris* brought by Defendants, and who poffibly might have delay for their object. Upon running over the Statutes of James the Firft, and William and Mary, made in England, with regard to *Certioraris*, it appears that thefe Writs may be iffued either in term time by the Court, or with certain regulations by a Puifne Judge in vacation This fhews they are not original Writs. —If a Puifne Judge in his Chambers, had the power of iffuing original Writs, I fancy certain officers of Chancery would feel a fenfible decreafe of their profits A book (not of much authority I confefs) *Bohun's Englifh Lawyer*— obferves that the *Certioraris* now in practice, whether granted by a Judge, or the Court, are rather Proceffes than Writs, and furely let the Rule in *Shower* be what it may, it could only bind the Court that made it, and could not make a law for the King's Bench of Ireland.

The next objection was, that the Prifoner ought to have been in Court on the day his trial was apppointed, for this the cafe of the *King* and *Johnfon* was cited ; this cafe is reported partly in *Fofter*, in *Strange*, and in the firft *Barnardiftu Spaifim* what relates to the prefent queftion is in page 111 ——*Kettelby*, the Prifoners counfel, moved the Court to appoint a day of trial , the

Court

Court refused him, as his case was not within the Statute which entitled a Prisoner to the aid of Counsel, and the Court observed further, that this application could not be made without the Prisoners being present, upon which *Kettelby* desired that the Court would grant a Rule to bring him up, and the Court did so —This is the whole of that case   The question then is, is it mere practice, or is the omission error ? It was said, if I recollect right, that he should have a *dies datus* , if so it must be part of the Record when made up , but upon examination, I do not find in the precedents any such entry, and in my opinion, the question about personal presence is a question of practice merely   In the case of the *King* and *Sprag*, and another, the Defendants were convicted at the assizes of a conspiracy, and the conviction had been removed by *Certiorari*, but not the persons.—The words in *Burrow* are—" The Court held this to be a fixed " and invariable *rule of practice in this Court*,"— that Defendants must be present, and it appears by the report of this same case in 1st. *Black. Rep* that the Court directed the Defendants Counsel to move for a *Habeas Corpus* to bring him up the second day of the next Term, and which by the way shews, that there was nothing in the objection, as to the Return of the *Habeas Corpus* not being on a general-day   If this therefore, was but a question of practice, the Court, in my mind, might dispense with it Here the Court had been applied to by the Prisoner's Counsel, on Saturday June the twenty-third, to remand the Record and suspend the *Habeas Corpus* which had been applied for and granted the sixteenth ——— Affidavits were read of the Prisoner's ill state of health, and that the bringing them up would in-

U   danger

Rex versus K-on.
7 Wm 3 ch. 3

2 Bur 930.

209.

Rex
verfus
K.on.

danger their (or fome of their) lives—it would
therefore have had the appearance rather of cru-
el'y to bring them up in that Term, however, I
will not fay but that if the want of perfonal prefence were error, the Prifoners counfel had a
right to infift upon it, even though it arofe from
indulgence.

The laft two points, I mean as to the Return
of the *Venire* and the feverance of the pannel,
I own appeared to me, to be of much difficulty.
—I have examined them with all the care I
could. I confidered the motion in arreft of judgment, not an application to our difcretion, not
to be influenced by applications to the paffions,
but a *Demand of a Right*, in the prefent cafe the
demand not of a rich man, but however the demand of a man *intitled* in common with all other
fuitors, to *call* upon the Judges of the land, at
the proper feafon, *jus dicere*.

6 St. Tr.
4 St Tr
6 Mod
Tutchin's
Cafe.

What is faid by Chief Juftice *Pratt* in *Layer's*
trial, and by *Holt* in the other two cafes quoted
from the State Trials, fhews clearly that thefe
Judges thought they ought not deviate from the
practice: But *Layer's* cafe is in my mind, far
from being free from confufion In the begin-
ning of the cafe Chief Juftice *Pratt* is made to
fay, that he could not appoint any day but a
general return without making error in the
proceedings The Prifoner had begged for a few
days, which one would fuppofe could not be
given even by confent; and yet afterwards when
the queftion came in arreft of judgment, he does
not anfwer the objections of the Prifoners counfel, but applies to the officer for the practice;
and it there appears that although the Return
was on a general day, the trial muft be not on
that day, but the *quarto die poft*. I rather think
it

it would have been more properly called the day of appearance.

See what the *quarto die post* of the first Return is this year, *Hillary* begining Monday, 4°. Wednesday ——*Easter* the like ——*Trinty* Monday, 4°. Friday.——*Michaelmas*, Monday, 4°. Thursday—What can a jury do? Is it not better to have the trial the day of the Return? If it be but a question of practice I must decide in favour of ours. There were but three Return days on which trials could be had in *Michaelmas Term*. The case of *Newburgh* and *Burrows*, ran through two of these days, and then we should have had but one day for all the other trials at bar— There is a good reason why there should be fifteen days between the Teste and Return, when a cause comes in from a foreign county, but I see none for fixing the trial invariably to the *quarto die post* —If it be but practice in *Westminster-Hall*, our practice may vary—The rules might have been formed from different reasons, and which did not extend to both kingdoms —'Tis true, we adopted the laws of England in the reign of *Henry* VII but we never indiscriminately repealed the Irish acts which had passed before that time, that were not contrariant to 10 *Henry* VII —Where a matter is sanctioned by usage immemorial, one may go so far as to presume an Ordinance, or even a Statute, although the Roll be not now to be found.—The old English Statutes of *Westminster*, *Gloster*, *Merton*, and *Marlebridge*, are not to be found on the Rolls, they are now only to be met with in printed books —The usage of the Courts of Ireland has even in *Westminster-Hall* been often attended to upon Writs of Error, and it appears in *Strange*, that they have attended to certificates made by Irish Judges,

in

Rex
versus
Keon.

Rex
verſus
Keon.

in one caſe by the Chancellor, two Chief Juſtices, the Chief Baron, and four Judges

I confeſs I had ſome doubts how queſtions of practice could be made queſtions in a Court of Error. In many points our own Courts differ, for example, it appeared by a caſe a few days ago, that this Court differs from the Court of *Common Pleas* in the recognizance of bail. Suppoſe Writs of Error from two Courts, differing in practice, went to the Houſe of Lords; what would that Court do? would it direct an iſſue, or condeſcend to ſend for, and examine the Clerks? Thinking it therefore but practice, and finding from our Officer, that as far as can be traced, we have had the Returns on days certain, I think this objection muſt be diſallowed.

As to the laſt point, I mean ſevering the pannel, or rather the trial, my doubt was how the Record could be made up, and whether the iſſue not being found as to the other four, it was not a diſcontinuance, and which, if ſo, I think would extend to the Priſoner at the bar, as well as to the others

1 Jon.
367 Cr.
Car 426

I think the caſe of *Tyſſen* verſus *Turton*, ſhews that there need not be any ſurmiſe before verdict—Here it is ſtronger—This indictment is in fact a ſeparate charge againſt each—the guilt of one is not the guilt of the others, the facts, the evidence may be different, the arraignment is ſeveral they pleaded ſeverally, and the finding of the Jury muſt be taken ſeverally, and not joint 'Tis not like the caſe of *Conſpiracy*, and ſome others, where the facts of ſeveral amount to a joint crime; but here *A* may be convicted of murder, *B* of manſlaughter, and *C* may have a ſpecial a special verdict found against him, stating facts which may cause great doubts whether he ought to be convicted at all. It seems still to be a matter of some doubt, how far a man within signal, but at a *distance and out of sight*, may be charged as present. But to resume the point about making up the Record, in the *King* v *Royce*, where a cause had been removed by *Certiorari*, the Court of King's Bench gave judgment without calling upon the defendant to plead *de novo* below, as it is contended for we ought to have done, and for which that wretched case in Carthew, *Tabula in Naufragio*, the *King* v *Baker*, was cited. The same point appears in the *King* v *Sprag* already mentioned, and in the *King* v *Royce*. The fourth objection there was, that it did not appear from the Record then in Court, what had been done with two others who had been jointly indicted, and some old cases were quoted, but the answer was, the cases of the defendants were distinct and separate —Although *there Royce* was only charged as a principal in the second degree.

In truth, if there have been any irregularities, most of them were done in favour of the Prisoner, and by the indulgence of the Counsel for the Crown, he was allowed *Oyer* of the *Venire* and *Return*, to which he was not entitled, but which the Crown did not refuse, he was allowed to make challenges for non-residence, which if objected to, must have been refused. But I incline to think he has waived his time for objecting, he moved to put off his trial upon affidavit, but never mentioned any objection, save these in his affidavit, he challenged the Return of the *Venire*, and prayed that the Return and Pannel might be quashed, he then challenged

Rex versus Keen

4 Bur. 2073 2085.

6 Carth.

Bur. 2085

Rex
verjus
Keon,

3 Atk.
357.

Pa. 86.

lenged the Polls   Lord *Hardwicke* fays that
in the cafe of *Whittington* and *Charlton* (which
was an appeal of murder) it was determined
that the parties appearance had cured an irregularity in *mefne* procefs.   Three Judges, *Par-
ker*, *Powis* and *Eyre*, were of this opinion, *John
Powel* contra   I fought for this cafe, 'tis imper-
fectly reported in 10 *Mod.* and is mentioned in
Hawkins, *Strange*, and *Salkeld.*   If this be the
rule of law, the unfortuhate man at the bar has
paffed his time for availing himfelf, little or much
as the advantage may be, of any irregularity that
has happened   As to the queftion whether there
be Error or not in this cafe, I take great confolation from what has fallen from his own Counfel,
of an intention to apply for a Writ of Error —If
we are right, our opinion will be confirmed by
men of great abilities and eftablifhed character.
—If wrong, thank God we can do no harm.

[During the whole of the motion in Arreft of
Judgment, the Prifoner fat at the bar attended
by a Clergyman —As foon as the Court had
pronounced their decifion on that motion,]

The *Clerk of the Crown* faid—Prifoner ftand
up at the bar, and hold up your right hand.

Which the Prifoner having done,

Clerk of the Crown —Robert Keon, you have
been heretofore indicted for that you not having the fear of God before your eyes, nor the
duty of your allegiance confidering, but being
wholly moved and feduced by the inftigation of
the devil, on the 16th day of October, in the
twenty-fixth year of his Majefty's reign, at Drynaun in the county of Leitrim, did traitoroufly
kill

kill and murder George Reynolds, otherwife called George Nugent Reynolds, by difcharging at him a piftol charged with gunpowder and leaden bullets, and thereby giving him a mortal wound upon the head, a little above the left eyebrow, of which he inftantly died, againft the peace and ftatute —Upon this indictment you have been arraigned, and on your arraignment pleaded not guilty, and for trial put yourfelf upon God and your country, which country formerly found you guilty, and thereupon Counfel on your behalf moved the Court in Arreft of the Judgment, and the Court is now unanimoufly of opinion, that the Judgment againft you ought not to be arrefted What have you now, therefore, to fay for yourfelf why judgment of death and execution thereupon fhould not be awarded againft you according to law?

And the prifoner having faid nothing, Lord *Earlfort* proceeded

Earlsfort, C J.—It becomes a very neceffary though very painful part of my duty, as well for the example of others, as for your good, to ftate fome of the circumftances of the black fact of which you have been found guilty by a refpectable Jury of your own county, and in truth as refpectable a Jury as any other country could produce —You have been found guilty of MURDER—the moft horrible offence that is to be found in the catalogue of human crimes—and in this cafe attended with circumftances of aggravation.—As many of the public attend on this occafion, it becomes neceffary to ftate the facts

facts; and perhaps it is in a certain degree *perſonal*, when I reflect that you are an attorney, and an officer of our Court, who from your age and your ſituation, muſt have been apprized of the conſequences

It ſeems, the unhappy victim of your reſentment had uſed ſome aſperſive language with regard to you, and you took the moſt ſummary and moſt violent mode of ſatisfying your own anger, and vindicating your feelings of falſe honour—You, an Attorney, ſought the moſt public place, the county town, the ſitting the Judges, to publicly beat him, one would have thought human wrath could not have gone farther; one would have thought, that the perſon who tamely received ſuch an inſult could have excited no other paſſion but pity, and have overcome every thing like reſentment.

To ſatisfy the world, to ſatisfy the falſe appearances of honour, Mr. Reynolds ſent a common friend to you, who apprized you, that you might appear as an adverſary without any fear of danger to you, for that Mr Reynolds would have no weapon to do you miſchief Whether this previous notice were agreed to or not, on your part, is of little importance—If it were, it was the moſt abominable treachery—if not, it was puſillanimity and horrid reſentment—After ſuch a propoſal, you went on the next day, after having ſlept a night, after having, as every man muſt be ſuppoſed to have done, addreſſed yourſelf to the Almighty in prayer, and ruſhed in the moſt brutal manner on the wretched object of your rage, and deprived him of his life, nor even then ſatisfied, while the wretch lay dead at your feet, you continued to expreſs your reſentment.

It muft be a great addition to what you en-
dure, to feel that you have drawn a long family
into the moft diftrefsful fituation, by this fad indulgence of your paffions—I am fure I feel much
for them. But there is one confolation that I
have, that though there has been a long delay
given to juftice in your cafe, yet it ferves to
fhew, that no man, however entrenched in
wealth and connections, but will find the law
too ftrong for his crimes

You have had every affiftance the law could
afford you, and I truft that it has given you time
to make fome attonement to that Power whom
you feem to have fo long forgotten

His Lordfhip then proceeded to pronounce the
judgment as in cafes of High Treafon.

1 H H
P C 750,
751, 382
2 H H
P C 356,
397

The Prifoner was ordered for execution on the
16th day of February following, and a *Writ* for
that purpofe was iffued, under the feal of the
Court of King's Bench, and not the ordinary
Warrant, as at Affizes and Seffions.

The WRIT was in the following words

* GEORGE the Third, by the Grace of God of Great
Britain, France and Ireland, King Defender of the Faith, and
foforth To the Sheriffs of the county of the city of Dublin,
greeting —Whereas Robert Keon, hath been by due form of
law, attainted of traiteroufly killing and murdering George
Nugent Reynolds, in the county of Leitrim; It is thereupon
confidered by the Court here, that the faid Robert Keon be
taken from the Bar of the Court where he now ftands, to the
place from whence he came, (the gaol) that his irons are to be
ftruck off, and from thence he is to be drawn to the place of
execution, (the gallows) and there he is to be hanged by the
neck, but not until he is dead, for whilft he is yet alive he is
to be cut down, his bowels are to be taken out and burned,
and he being yet alive, his head is to be fevered from his body,
his body is to be divided into four quarters, and his head and
quarters are to be at his Majefty's difpofal —The execution of
which judgment remaineth yet to be done —We therefore require,

X

Rex
verſus
Keon.

The Counſel for the Crown on this trial and motion in Arreſt of Judgment, in the Court above, were,

Henry Duquery,
William Caldbeck,
John Philpot Curran,
Chriſtopher Stone Williams,
John Kirwan,   } Eſqrs.
John Geoghegan,
Gerald O'Farral,
George Joſeph Browne,
And George Moore,

Solicitor for the Proſecution Mr. Ch. J. Niſbitt

The Priſoners Counſel on the trial and motion in Arreſt of Judgment, were,

James Fitzgerald, Eſq, his Majeſty's Prime Serjeant,
The Honourable Joſeph Hewitt, his Majeſty's Third Serjeant,

The

quire, and by theſe preſents, ſtrictly command you, that upon the ſixteenth day of February next, you repair to the ſaid gaol, and thereout take the body of the ſaid Robert Keon, and him ſo taken out in ſafe cuſtody, you are to convey to the accuſtomed place of execution in your ſaid county of the city of Dublin, and that you on that day do cauſe execution to be done upon the ſaid Robert Keon, in all things as herein before are particularly mentioned, and this you are by no means to omit at your perils ——Witneſs *John, Lord Earlsfort*, at the King's Courts, the 31ſt day of January, in the twenty-eighth year of our reign.

CARTER.

By the Court—for the King.

Exd by J. BRADSHAW, *D. C. C.*

(COPY.)

CPSIA information can be obtained
at www.ICGtesting.com
Printed in the USA
BVHW022253310123
657600BV00007B/101

9 781275 309951